THE IMPROBABLE PROFESSOR

Reflections of a Reluctant Reductionist

HOWARD M. STIEN

Of the making of books there is no end;
And much learning is weariness of the flesh.

ECCLESIASTES 5:6

What the heck, one more can't hurt!

© 2003 Howard M Stien
First published in 2003 by Stump House Books
ISBN: 0-9707334-1-0

All Rights Reserved. No part of this publication may be reproduced, stored in a retrieval system, or transmitted in any form or by any means, electronic, mechanical, photocopying, recording, or otherwise, except for purposes of critical review, without the express written permission of the copyright owner.

For information you may contact Howard Stien at
Stump House Books: 11411 N Pinecrest Drive
Spokane, WA 99218.

Published by Stump House Books
Spokane, WA 99218, USA
1 509 466-5994

Cover design - Pauline Haas, Spokane WA
Book design - Kindred Creative Services, St. Paul, MN
Printed in the USA

Dedication

For all my students at Migh College and the University of Yores who taught me well

Gretchen - Alice - Paul - Bob - Peter - David - Jim - Cheryl - Pati - Brad
Ted - Mike - Chris - Kristy - Stan - Sten - Brian - Dan - Barb - Ingrid
Mimi - Zach - Bryce - Don - Gil - Nick - Mark - Joe - Rick - Eric - Kim
Diane - Byron - Dennis - George - Steve - Beth - Clyde - Jennifer - Roy
Paul - Jesse - Dana - Walt - Jan - Roger - Marshal - Carol - Pam - Susan
Primal - Liz - Nancy - Janis - K-E - Bruce - Phil - Larry - Ed - Chuck
Kathy - Shaunda - Heather - Joanne - Tim - Penny - Phoebe - Doug
Sandra - Terry - Laura - Ken - Randy - Jerred - Gordon - Jeanne - Mark
Rod - Signe - Wendy - Gerry - Val - Keith - Craig - Gaylan - Jack - Jeff
Ray - Dave - Sheryl - Dale - Riley - Heidi - Robin - Julie - Katie - Loren
Suzanne - Faith - Kevin - Forest - Scott - Mad - Abbie - Tony - Tad
Carolyn - Annette - Karl - Sylvia - Jody - Malia - Sam - Amanda
Brandon - Brent - Mandy - Troy - Jill - Kyrsten - Denise - Kendra
Justin - Toni - Colleen - Lori - Ara - Lynn - Robyn - Foster - Art - Vickie
Shauna - Marcia - Vincent - Todd - Cinda - Connie - Anna
Mohammed - Alan - Clara - Hal - Kelley - Debra - Carrie - Carla
Karin - Ketra - Gary - Harvey - Janine - Kent - Coleen - Laurel - Chrystal
Nikki - Kristina - Meredith - Samantha - Patti - Alida - Ryan - Guy
April - Britta - Kathi - Jon - Hydi - Kari - Keisha - Tara - Mindy
Karla - Kebra - Travis - Trevor - Pat - Corey - Tanya - Rip - Teri - Kurt
Keiran - Doragail - Ada - Kristine - Janae - Janelle - Monica - Jayme
Gwen - Chip - Gwyn - Kirsten - LaRae - Mary - Judith - Marty - Sandy
Wanda - Terri - Monty - Brita - Stephanie - Cornelius - Andrea - Jenny
Laurie - Theresa - Kevin - Jonathon - Stacy - Sidney - Marc - Melissa
Autumn - Watts - Marvin - Elaine - Cydney - Darlene - Peggy - Michelle
Lindy - Samatha - Brandy - Rachel - Brett - Cindy - Sarah - Jeanee
Marquis - Martina - Oscar - Frieda - Norman - Agnes - Violet - Jordan

Contents

Foreword by Dr Darrell Guder and Dr. Lisa Sardinia ix

Prologue 3
A Premonition 5
It's in the Making 9
Predestination 13
Masters of Minutiae............................. 19
Didn't Get the Memo........................... 23
Dubious Distinction............................27
Undone... 31
Professorial Preoccupations..................... 35
Reluctant Readers 41
Perquisites Pertaining Thereto 45
A Manner of Speaking........................... 51
Meeting of the Minds........................... 57
Deans, Deaning & Deanlets..................... 61
Fabrication....................................... 67
The Meritocracy................................. 73
Rank Ritualism.................................. 77
Perils of Peerlessness 81
Death by Degree................................. 85
Academic Circles................................ 89
Managed Mussiness............................. 93
Believe It... 97
Idea Merchants 103
Divine Diversion................................ 107
Molecular Me 111
Probabilities..................................... 115
The Right Not to Write......................... 121
Student Teachers................................ 125
Acknowledgements 131

Foreword

The purpose of a foreword is, I think, to commend a book to its readers, and perhaps to point out some particular reasons to engage the book's arguments and its author. During my tenure as "one of the many deans in whose training [Howard Stien] has had a part" (p. 125), I gladly commend this volume to what I hope will be a very broad circle of readers.

For past students, this literary visit with the "improbable professor" will refresh memories of their encounters with one of the most notable and influential personalities of their campus years.

For past and present colleagues, these reflections and ruminations will continue the conversations that, over the years, delighted, frustrated, provoked, and invariably stimulated – conversations about every aspect of our common calling in perhaps the most distinctive expression of American educational culture, the small liberal arts college.

For future teachers and new professors, this book is a valuable but also sobering survey of the realities and fantasies of our academic existence – a healthy dose of common sense that will greatly benefit the guild.

And for everyone, it simply a good read, full of delights, surprises, and insights that will hook themselves into one's mind and prod one to muse and wonder about things one has not quite seen that way before.

The dedication of the book, "for all my students," is the key to reading it with full appreciation. This is a book by a man called and gifted to teach, energized by the educational encounter in classroom, office, and laboratory, and unswervingly focused on the priority he placed upon his students, their learning, and their general welfare. It is no surprise to read at the end of the book that what he misses, in retirement, are his students. Although he intimidated them (I am persuaded that he learned the art of intimidation and practiced it with great skill for good pedagogical reasons), challenged them, in his candor and forthrightness at times took their breath away, they always knew that they and their full development into the people they were meant to be was what mattered most to him.

After a commencement ceremony at which we had been blessed with an unusually long-winded address by the invited speaker, Howard said to me that our guest "had missed several wonderful opportunities to stop." It is good for all of us that Howard has not stopped even though retired, that is, has not stopped thinking about the remarkable pilgrimage of his life, its serendipities and struggles, its possible meaning, and its as yet unanswered questions. It is no surprise that he does so with that wit and honesty that at times may cause us to flinch but always cause us to think.

Darrell L. Guder, PhD.

Sometime vice-president of academic affairs and dean of the faculty at Whitworth College. Currently the Henry Winters Luce Professor of Missional and Ecumenical Theology at Princeton Theological Seminary

A student's perspective

And from Lisa Sardinia, J.D., PhD.

Associate Professor of Biology at Pacific University

Early in my college career I enrolled in a four-week freshman biology course offered by Professor Stien, my assigned academic advisor. At the time I was convinced of two things: biology was not high on my list of academic interests and Stien's reputation for candor and academic rigor were disquieting at the very least.

But my emerging intellectual curiosity overruled my trepidation and I stayed the course. By the end of the term I knew two new things: Stien's demeanor and pedagogical style were the stuff of which legends are made and I actually wanted to study biology – "an essential component of an informed world view," as Professor Stien would argue.

Except for a passion for biology, Stien and I would seem to have little in common. (I never wanted to be a farmer.) But here I am, a biology professor at another quality liberal arts college. Like Stien (and possibly because of him) my path has not been linear. Five classes with Stien freed me to ponder bigger questions, the ones that couldn't be answered by spending my life researching the protein processing of coronaviruses – my contribution to knowledge. In addition to biology I completed advanced studies in another discipline because I could not fully immerse myself in the minutiae of molecular biology. After that my only option was obvious – become a professor!

I can't say I've modeled my teaching style after Stien (I don't wear black to exams), but I am certainly still asking "Stien-like" questions to help clear the peripheral vision of my students. Maybe that's the similarity among us "improbable" professors. Without abdicating our allegiance to our first academic love, we rejected the blinders offered us by our graduate programs and made room in our minds for other avenues of thought.

With insight and wit Dr. Stien unveils the fantasies and foibles of the professoriate. I think all of his students and everyone else who reads The Improbable Professor will be affirmed in their endeavors to avoid one-dimensional intellectual lives. Stien is correct – it can be done. His story and my experience attest to that.

THE IMPROBABLE PROFESSOR

Reflections of a Reluctant Reductionist

Prologue

The right to write is a fundamental professorial prerogative and the penultimate professorial triumph is to write a book. The ultimate, of course, is to publish it. Surely professionals other than professors write books, but they write for different reasons. For instance, some write because they have something to say. Others write because they know how to do it well enough to get paid. Novel motivation.

But most professors write books because the deans and other professors pester them to do so. Unfortunately, many of us are too easily persuaded that anyone – especially professors – given a little discipline and some quiet time can write and that fame and fortune and, perhaps, promotion await those who do.

The nouns *professor* and *writer* are not necessarily synonymous, which doesn't readily occur to most professors, and we are too easily convinced that being professors not only enables us to write but gives us permission to do so.

Nonetheless, emboldened by the tradition and not wanting to be found wanting by my fellow professors, I have given myself permission to write this *otherwise unauthorized* account of what I've learned about professors during my tenure among the ranks of the noble profession at Migh College and the University of Yores.

Premonition

Professor was not on my boyhood list of things I wanted to be when I grew up. Professors simply were not part of the real world in which I lived as a boy. My domain was a depression and drought-plagued dust bowl farm in western Minnesota during the dirty thirties. My father was a farmer. I wanted to be a farmer.

My Danish immigrant grandfather was also a farmer. Although he never said so, I suspect he wanted to be a professor. He had names for all of his grandchildren, names other than those assigned by their parents. He called me *The Perfesser* and when he called me that it sounded more like accusation than affirmation. I remember being envious of my brother whom he called "the truck driver." Why my grandfather called me *The Perfesser* and how that influenced my becoming one I will never know.

"Be a perfesser," my grandfather would say in his delightful Danish accent. "It beats working for a living. It's nice clean inside work and – apart from some weighty ideas – there's no heavy lifting." It was only because of his chatter about them that I knew there were people called professors. Beyond that I gave them little thought before I entered my first college class.

5

My grandfather's premonition notwithstanding, I had no intention of becoming a professor when I first went to college. In fact, that I went to college at all was an enigma to my immigrant parents. They were schooled in the old-world notion that the natural order of life for a son was to follow the craft of his father. Consequently, my parents thought of my brothers and me as carpenters and farmers. I served my apprenticeship in both vocations before I went to college. Looking back I find it quite remarkable, even improbable, that I could have anticipated a professorial career having come of age in those rather modest circumstances and with a persistent allegiance to that heritage.

My mother, a sturdy Danish woman, taught us well her prescription for a good life: work hard, stay out of trouble, keep yourself clean, and be good to others whenever you can. "None of that requires a college education," she would say.

I tried to become a farmer. But a $2,000 education was easier to come by than a $200,000 farm. (This was 1950.) So setting aside that dream, I left the farm at the advanced age of twenty-seven to go to college for the first time. I stayed in college the next ten years, taking courses and observing professors and, in the end, received the third degree. (The number of degrees earned establishes ones potential to be a professor as well as license to be one.) Although it was not why I went to college, I was a professor before I realized it.

Now I *still* want to be a farmer, but before I dust off that dream I want to reflect on my four-decade diversion into the professoriate, perchance to discover what my grandfather anticipated but never told me.

Some folks believe that the longer one does something the less inclined or capable one is to do something else. That could be true. I have been a professor most of my adult life. But I don't think I ever became totally comfortable doing what many professors do – that is, taking money for professing obviosities to unsuspecting young people and providing them answers to questions they have not yet asked. I may have entered the arena not totally convinced that "professing" was a legitimate way of making a living. I do recall there were times when my grandfather called me *The Perfesser* he seemed to suggest that all was not well with me.

It's in the Making

Of the making of professors there seems to be no end. Ever wonder what prompts someone to become a professor? It is generally thought by the working world that professors can't do anything else. My grandfather often said so. While that may be true, it doesn't explain how they get that way.

There are no university courses that teach one how to become a professor. I don't think young people enter college intending to become professors. There are pre-medical, pre-law, pre-seminary programs, but I never encountered a *pre-professor* curriculum. I think professors are accidental by-products of a system that is intended to educate people. The process has become diverted and is a good example of the means becoming the end. I haven't decided whether my becoming a professor was something I did or something done to me. I am nagged by the thought that it may have just happened.

Something does happen to people on their way to becoming professors, which eventually differentiates us from ordinary folks. It has more to do with how we think than what we look like. I cannot clearly recall the moment before which I was not a professor and after which I, irrevocably, was one. The transition is imperceptible – usually not evident to those to whom it is happening. Faculty appointments or tenure have little to do with it, nor does accumulating a certain prescribed minimum of knowledge. I know many knowledgeable people who are not professors. My father was one and he was a farmer.

Certainly professors are informed persons – more informed than ordinary folks, perhaps, but most likely in areas of little interest to anyone other than themselves and their disciples. What happens, I think, is that we professors begin to think too much about our significance in the world. I am suspicious that we unwittingly come to believe the world works primarily in ways that are consonant with the fabrications of whatever guild licensed us and we feel obliged to say so. The extent to which we master and become comfortable with the constructs of our guild is taken as evidence that we are ordained to be professors *with all the rights and privileges pertaining thereto.*

I would think no graduate student could forget the vexation of having to compromise one's intellectual independence to earn the privilege to write under the guidance of the guild in which he or she was apprenticing. But that is probably the very point at which they relinquish their freedom to think otherwise. It becomes nearly impossible to see over the fences that screen our minds from other ways of understanding.

The initiation process is subtly pervaded with expectations that one will become like the master professor under whose tutelage the trek began. That should be the would-be professor's first warning for that's how professors beget professors. When trafficking in ideas (apart from becoming professors) what else is there to do?

I'm afraid my ambivalence about whether being a professor was the most judicious way for me to have spent my life shows more than I want it to. Perhaps I am reluctant to leave the impression that I was incapable of doing anything else. I apprenticed long enough as a soldier, truck driver, farmer, and carpenter on the way to becoming a professor to qualify for employment in any of those crafts. But none of those activities did much to ease my curiosity about how the world works. Thinking that was the purpose of education, I set out in search of understanding about how the world functions only to discover four decades later that much of the time it doesn't work the way we professors think it does. On the way I became a professor.

To the extent that it is possible for a professor to do so, I think of myself as an ordinary guy (which may not be fair to ordinary folks). I go about the tasks of living in much the same way that ordinary folks do. I eat, sleep, breathe and participate in all the necessary biological rituals of life. I go to work. I love, care for and tease my wife and children as much or as little as anyone.

Like ordinary folks, I participate in many of the socially acceptable recreational and cultural rites of civilized society. I go to church, attend symphony concerts and football games. I talk to my wife. I read books and watch TV. I laugh and cry and get along reasonably well with ordinary folks (my kind of people) and I don't intentionally advertise the fact that I am a professor.

But something usually betrays me. It is not because I feel obliged to answer every question I hear, a proclivity of some professors I know. Nor is it that I do a lot of talking, another professorial propensity. It could be that I do a lot of thinking, but so did my father and he was a farmer.

Maybe Grandfather was right.

Predestination

The degree to which a professor's self-esteem is dependent upon his or her academic credentials is something students will want to know. Careful students of classroom protocol learn quickly what a professor prefers to be called. No doubt students have all sorts of names for their professors, which may be used everywhere on campus except in the presence of the professor being addressed.

In students' encounters with professors there are points to be gleaned by the careful exploitation of a professor's personal investment in titles. "What shall I call you? Is it Doctor or Mister?" students ask. That, I soon learned, was not an effort to learn the extent of my formal education. They could have learned that from the college catalogue. But rather it was an attempt to detect my susceptibility to flattery. In negotiations about final grades that were not up to a student's expectations, a little flattery is more effective than an adversarial posture. And given professors' investment in titles, it certainly doesn't help to call a professor by a title to which he or she is not entitled.

In the contemporary erosion of classroom formality, students employ a strategy of familiarity. This works well with profs named Bob or Bill or some other harmless moniker that can't be made to carry an innuendo.

But my name is Howard. And despite the fashion of using a professor's first name, there is something about Howard that seemed to cause my students to be apologetic for calling me that.

I am not sure what all this has to do with my having been a professor, except that I wonder why my students found it difficult to call me Howard. Not once in forty years in the profession did a student address me by my given name. Perhaps they recognized that having been named Howard is something one never gets over and they wished not to call attention to that.

My parents never did apologize for calling me Howard and they were the ones who did it first. In fact, my father once said that he was glad they named me Howard because everyone called me that anyway. I wonder whether they may have had some premonition about it and could not have done otherwise.

The birth of a child is seldom a surprise. The real surprise comes not to the parents but to the children when they first realize what their parents chose to name them. The child arrives and, if all is well with the mother and baby, the first significant decision that the parents will probably make is what this child shall be called. Strangely, there are no rules regulating this most serious responsibility (except ironically, in Norway, the birthplace of my father). There may be traditions or customs, but there are no binding rules. One wonders why such a grave oversight has gone uncorrected in our society.

The way it stands, parents are allowed absolute freedom to label their newborn with whatever tag pleases them and usually with little regard for the effect it may have on the child. If there is any rational discourse in the process, it will likely be a debate about which of two equally non-rational choices should prevail.

Psychologists and sociologists have studied every circumstance, both real and imaginary, believed to account for one's personality or lack thereof. But I know of no study designed to explore the burdens imposed on children by inappropriate names. I wonder why it has not occurred to these analysts of personality that a child's life is doomed to disquiet of all kinds the moment it realizes how casually its parents have exercised their first responsibility. Unfortunately, by the time one realizes that the name assigned by one's parents is the root of all one's troubles it is too late to undo the damage and one's destiny is determined. It has been said that one becomes what one is named. Given my grandfather's premonition, it seems I was destined to become a professor named Howard.

My parents obviously knew that my mother was about to give birth. What they didn't know was that there were two of us. So they were unexpectedly confronted with a double dilemma. Not only did they have to contend with two babies, they had to choose two names. In fairness to my parents I must admit that they had given some thought to names prior to the surprise. But the shock of twins seems to have momentarily confused their thinking.

It was their intention to name their first male child Hans, which was, coincidentally, the name of both prospective grandfathers. That seemed rational enough. They could have named both of us Hans, which interestingly is discouraged even in the absence of rules.

What they did instead was retain the first letter of Hans and select names from a list that begin with the letter H. It doesn't require literary genius to know that the list of names beginning with H is not prime nomenclature. What healthy kid wants to answer to Hubert, or Henry, or Humphrey, or Hugh, or Hector, or Herman, or Helmut? I suppose I should be grateful that the list included Harold and Howard – which now, curiously, seem to be the least unacceptable – because that's what they decided we should be named.

Wearied by that decision my parents were unable to decide which of the two of us should be named Howard. So they asked my Danish grandfather, Hans, who had come to assess this twin phenomenon. "That one looks like a professor, call him Howard," he said pointing to me. "Name the other one Harold. He looks like a politician." (My hat size was always larger than his.) He did become a politician, a good one. He had a talent for the impossible.

From then on we were Harold and Howard, never Howard and Harold even though I was born first. I don't suppose I can blame my parents for that, but always when we were seen together folks would say, "There's Harold and his brother." It seems that from the beginning not only was I was destined to be a professor but one whose identity was relative.

Masters of Minutiae

To make a contribution to knowledge is an expectation we professors impose upon ourselves. In fact, it's a major rite of passage into the profession to do just that. This expectation drives scholars to devote their lives to rummaging through the accumulated minutiae about what someone has written about what someone has written about what someone wrote (usually Plato, Shakespeare, or the Bible). The standard procedure is to read the latest fifty books about some event or person and write yet another book.

The number of books written about books is unbelievable. This is called research: an exercise in trivialization which beginners are expected to master. These trivialities accumulate in journals and books, which are not widely read and have little value other than demonstrating to students how it is done.

Consequently, aspiring scholars become apprentices put to work in the master's shop learning the trade while extending the margins of the master's ideological domain. The invitation to participate requires intelligence, discipline, patience, some susceptivity to flattery, and is quite seductive. To keep their shops open, the master professors are obliged to cultivate a following of loyal students who think like they do. These converts (not prepared to do anything else) become professors sustaining the tradition. In their searches for an area about which something is still unknown, budding scholars are sent by their tutors down ever-narrowing pathways that soon become one-way streets. The seekers are not cautioned to look for the line beyond which their vision becomes restricted to one direction. Turning around becomes not only impossible but unthinkable. The investment in time and the cost in intellectual flexibility are too great.

I endured these rites of passage as a necessary requisite for recognition as an intellectual and I know that it is not easy to become a master of minutiae. One has to be bright enough to do it, but naïve enough to believe it has merit in itself. The outcome, nonetheless, is another professor.

When I began college nearly ten years older then my first-year classmates. I was mature enough to have learned that the purpose of education was more than learning how to do something (learning how to teach, or to practice law or medicine, or to be a professor). Education is not about spawning minutiae, which is only a rite of passage. It is about managing minutiae into some broader understanding of existence.

Ideas, I suppose, have to be about something whether that something be real or illusory. My decision about what fragment of the unknown I might uncover as my contribution to knowledge was influenced by my intrigue with the phenomenon of life in all of its manifestations. My rural heritage intruded into the decision. I chose biology because I was more at ease with ideas about real things — living things. Minutiae is minutiae and, while mastering minutiae about real things is no more virtuous than trafficking in the trivia of the abstruse, the former did keep my feet on the ground in the real world.

Like all aspiring scholars, I was challenged to find an area in which I might uncover some new bit of the unknown to submit as my contribution to knowledge. My offering — a bit of minutia about when in the ontogeny of liver tissue in chickens a species-specific protein can be detected — lies buried in the Journal of Fowl Comments in the library at the University of Yores.

Does anyone care? Probably not. Why anyone would want to know that is very likely the question most frequently asked about all the innumerable contributions to knowledge gathering dust somewhere. They do, nevertheless, demonstrate the mastery of minutiae or, as I prefer, the triumph of trivia.

Yet I have seldom encountered a professor who is not convinced that his or her bit of trivia is indispensable. To harbor misgivings about one's ideas can endanger a professor's livelihood. Maintaining the illusion that one's spin on the minutiae is crucial to the understanding of society is in a professor's personal and professional best interest. It is imperative that professors exploit all opportunities to impress society with their cerebrations.

And what better way to do that than to write books and to profess the scenario to a captive audience of young people. For professors to neglect or disavow their fabrications would leave them with nothing to talk about. They might have to go to work in the real world – a circumstance my grandfather would have applauded: a world which persists in all of its wholeness in spite of the efforts of professors to reduce it to abstractions.

Didn't Get the Memo

Writing memos was one of my favorite chores. Although no one has ever affirmed my opinion, I believe memos represent some of my most creative writing. It is imperative that professors learn not only how to write memos but also when it is in their best interest not to. Perhaps this is the only area where professors can be legitimately encouraged not to write. Occasionally I am reminded that some of my memos are still on file in the dean's office, a circumstance that could be cause for concern for untenured folks.

I submit my collection of memos and responses to them as evidence that I did, indeed, master the delicate art of memo writing. Some of my better memos were to colleagues who prefer the figurative meanings of words. With my limited skill in figuration, I found those not only quite challenging but also the most fun. Incidentally, there is no point in writing or receiving memos if one doesn't enjoy doing it.

Of course, memos should contain a message and that message should not exceed the recipient's capacity to get it. I have received some like that. *I didn't get the memo* doesn't necessarily mean one didn't receive it. Memos that don't say anything can be written quite unintentionally. They are much like sermons or philosophy lectures, which often say less than the author intended. Who more than philosophers say more than they need to? To intentionally write a memo that doesn't say anything, however, requires considerable skill.

Most folks enter the professoriate quite unschooled in the subtleties of memo writing. I know of no graduate school courses in this critical craft. Beginners would do well to submit to some mentoring by a master of the craft until they learn the difference between memos and mere notes. I realized the distinction when I received a note from the dean reminding me to take note of procedural protocol when addressing superiors. I apparently had failed to disguise my belief that there were none – superiors that is, not protocols.

The difference between notes and memos is subtlety, and those having trouble with the distinction should proceed with caution. A simple rule of thumb is that if the message is too readily understood it is probably a note. Memos are frequently written in a manner that challenges the recipient to understand what is to the writer a clear message.

The disposition of professors to believe that all sequences of words contain meaning – and their reluctance to admit they didn't understand – can be exploited by an expert memo writer. Few professors will seek assistance in deciphering a well-written memo, the message of which they didn't get. If a professor has reason to feel guilty, any memo (well written or not) will reinforce the feeling. The very same memo could cause a professor who thinks he or she has reason to feel good, to feel good. Unfortunately, when receiving a memo from the dean the latter experience is rare.

Memos should never be used to comfort complacency, especially those to administrators, who eventually get used to always being wrong. Memos need not be burdened with truth nor should they be employed to convey information. That is the function of notes. The domain of memos is impersonal, interpersonal affairs. Attitude, opinion, conviction, emotion, and wisdom are the stuff of which good memos are crafted. Most beginners would do well to defer the incorporation of wisdom to the wise. Good memos are those that will not be ignored and without which the genre would cease to exist.

Beginning a communication with MEMORANDUM does not, in itself, make the document a memo. It becomes a memo when it provokes a response. It is the reply that reveals what the recipient thought the message was and not infrequently gives the writer some insight about what he or she intended to say. My advice to young professors who may be uncertain of the intent of a memo is to ignore it, which (now that I think of it) may be the best response not only to most memos but to most anything written about them.

Dubious Distinction

Apart from my grandfather tagging me *The Perfesser*, there was no hint in my childhood or teenage years that I was destined to be a professor. That possibility absolutely never crossed my mind. I wanted to be a farmer. And given my parents' old-world traditions about sons following their fathers' vocations, no one ever discouraged that aspiration. Not even my grandfather, who continued to call me *The Perfesser* (a distinction I did not understand). I did become a farmer and, ironically, among my grandfather's twenty-eight grandchildren I was the only farmer. Interestingly, I am also the only professor.

Retirement, as we know it, had not yet been invented when my grandfather lived with us. Neither had Social Security. Folks who no longer worked lived with the younger generations who did. So my grandfather lived with us in the big farmhouse that had at one time been his. I never saw him engaged in chores or other farm work. Although he was no older then I am now, my recollection of him is of a bearded, white-haired, old fellow who read a lot and disagreed with everybody. His opinions were never humble and he voiced them freely and sometimes loudly on the streets of the county seat. Humility was not something I learned from him.

I never argued or disagreed with him. That as an option for young people also had not yet been imagined. Although he never engaged us, his grandchildren, in conversation he must have observed us. I wish I had asked him why he called me *The Perfesser*. On the other hand, I might not have liked his answer.

He died about the time I moved from the one-room, rural schoolhouse to high school in the county seat. If I were asked how my grandfather influenced my life, I wouldn't have an answer. We were all too busy surviving in those depression riddled, drought-stricken circumstances to contemplate the consequences of interpersonal relationships with adults. Trafficking in abstractions was not a luxury afforded either parents or kids doing chores on a dust bowl farm in the dirty thirties.

Tending the repository of society's abstractions is the prerogative of professors. Although my grandfather was not a professor, I suspect he preferred milking abstractions over helping us with the cows. He had his personal assemblage of abstractions, particularly those pertaining to politics, which he vigorously defended with a kind of blue-collar contempt for professional political pundits.

Family history reveals that my grandfather emigrated from Denmark under duress because of his opposition to the government's posture on labor unions. Incidentally, he was a carpenter then, not a farmer, and was fiercely involved in attempts to establish a carpenters union. I don't think my grandfather ever attained the status in society here that he enjoyed in Denmark. He seemed to harbor a resentment of intellectuals, especially those distant designers of public policy he categorized as professors.

My grandfather must have lived with some real dissonance. From my perspective as farm-boy observer he seemed to enjoy a good ideological scrap, all the while manifesting his peculiar Danish disdain for his imagined adversaries, the professors. Yet he called me *The Perfesser*. I prefer to think it was because I displayed some precocious talent for argument or abstraction. I can't believe it was because I talked too much. I wish I would have had occasion or the boldness to ask him, given his discord with idealists, why he called me *The Perfessor*. In retrospect, given his distrust, it seems at best a dubious distinction.

Undone

I remember my grandfather saying, after he was no longer able to work and had to busy himself with idleness, that the trouble with doing nothing was he never knew when he was done. Being a classroom professor is like that. At the end of the day professors have reasons to feel undone. Apart from self-acclaim, there are few ways for professors to measure their achievements at the end of the day.

To be sure some self-acclaim may be appropriate for those who have fabricated and published some small contribution to knowledge (which few people may read and fewer understand). But those persons are not really professors in the true sense of the word. They may be scholars, but they do very little professing and won't be nagged by doubts about whether what they professed mattered.

Most thoughtful professors who profess to students daily in the classroom begin to wonder if what they are professing really matters. It is that uncertainty which causes me to wonder at day's end whether my work is done. I used to cope by not thinking about it, but now I am older and need to know when it's time to quit.

A professor may know if his or her students are listening, which doesn't necessarily mean that what they are hearing matters much to them. That they took notes may mislead a novice to think it mattered – experienced professors know better. Taking notes is not the same as listening. Taking notes is like riding a bicycle. One has to do it to learn it, but once learned it can be done without thinking. I have known students who could take notes in their sleep. In fact, many students become very skilled at it.

Not only did I want my students to listen to me, I wanted them to hear what I was saying. The task is truly formidable. I am astounded at the audacity (or is it naiveté?) with which we professors face fifty students with fifty postures of expectation, indifference, confusion, confidence, fright, or acquiescence (thinking fifty different thoughts) and expect them all to hear the same thing or to hear anything at all. The final destiny of most lectures is, indeed, difficult to determine. Even the Bible admits that those who have ears to hear may not hear.

A common student response after hearing something which falls beyond the edges of what they already know (and which they often have judged to be sufficient) is: "Why do we have to know this?" My customary reply is: "So you will be able to talk intelligently with folks who do."

The next step after hearing is knowing *what* to know. Unfortunately, too often students seem to have concluded that the only use of knowledge is to answer test questions.

All too frequently they ask, "Is this something we should know?" Impending tests make it imperative that they know something, and exams are easier if they know what that is. However, this is precisely the point at which professors risk hindering the education of their students. Answering that question absolves the student of responsibility for thinking about what they have just heard and leaves the impression that knowing *per se* matters. It may matter but only until the test is finished and grades are posted. And when grades become the primary concern of the professors as well, they will have quit before their work is finished.

With only expressions of happy indifference on the faces of students to go by, professors can't know whether what they professed made any difference. If it is important to know at the end of a day what one accomplished, one should not become a professor because it won't be that way.

A major frustration of education is the lag time. Students can't help because they probably don't know yet whether it matters and perhaps won't for some time. The most I have come to expect of my lectures is that my students will remember what I said until the significance of it occurs to them. Fortunately, that happens for many, but that is of little comfort to the professor (or the dean) who needs to know the score at the end of the day.

Professorial Preoccupations

Of my Danish farmer grandfather's twenty-eight grandchildren I was the only one who seriously attempted a career in farming. It wasn't a lack of imagination about alternatives that nurtured my dream. Nor was it because no other encouraging opportunity beckoned.

When I was twelve a man with a tractor displaced my father and his horse-powered operation from the family farm. My father seemed relieved and glad to return to his preferred vocation of carpentry. But he had taught us well. I had learned to manipulate our huge draft horses and the field machinery they moved with ease. The smell of freshly plowed ground, the aroma of harvested grain, and the fragrance of new-mown hay still conjure nostalgic memories. My younger brothers were left with the less desirable routine chores with the livestock and the attending odors. Their olfactory recollections of boyhood farm life are less romantic.

Milking cows, harnessing horses, tending livestock, shoveling grain, pitching hay, gathering eggs, driving tractors, tilling fields, scooping manure, hoeing weeds, harvesting crops were all tasks we were expected to do and did from the time we were eight years old.

However, without a farm to farm these skills (now unused at home) were in demand by farmers attempting to operate their farms during a world war that drew most able-bodied young men off to defend the homeland. So my brothers and I, boys yet too young to go to war, were employed as "hired men" to keep out of mischief and to help support our family, now dependent on my father's carpentry. Three summers so employed concluded my apprenticeship as a farmer and strangely did little to dampen my determination to someday own and operate my own farm. But that was not to be, at least not until after another apprenticeship.

In the cultural milieu of World War II there were strong social incentives to join the fight, so I enlisted in The United States Army Air Corps. It was my ambition to serve as a bomber pilot, but I came along at a time when the military had more pilots in training than they had planes for them to fly. Inasmuch as six gunners were needed on each crew, there was no surplus of machine gunners. That became my assignment. In a few short months, still only eighteen years old and previously having been no farther than fifty miles from home, I was in Italy flying as the tail gunner on bombing missions over major European cities.

After the shooting had stopped and while waiting for my turn to be sent home, I was assigned to base personnel operations. It was there that I first encountered real professors, not the mythical ones at which my grandfather fumed. These were officers who, in their pre-military lives, had been psychology professors. They urged me to abandon my dream to become a farmer and go to college. They were, in my youthful judgment, competent at what they did and sincere in their interest in me. But they failed to convince me – they didn't know anything about farming.

While pursuing a short post-war career as a truck driver, I met a college-educated young woman, beautiful in person, spirit, and mind who came to teach at our local high school. Interestingly, she too had lived on a drought-imperiled, depression-threatened farm. Nevertheless, she was willing to risk fame and fortune and embark on the pursuit of my fantasy on her family's wheat farm.

We were young, healthy, optimistic, and ambitious. But the weather was arid, the soil marginal, our resources minimal, and our location isolated. Successful wheat growers in other parts of the country had flooded the market and prices were dismal. My preoccupation with farming was fast becoming a doubtful dream.

Before my mother began bearing and raising her family of seven, she taught children in one-room rural schools like the one we had attended. Although I was taught a healthy respect for teachers, I had never considered that an option for me. Hence, I was surprised to discover early in my farming venture that I was about to add teaching to my list of apprenticeships.

In the post-war years there was an unanticipated shortage of elementary school teachers to teach farm children in the many rural schools in our region. Former schoolteachers whose lives were interrupted by the war had gone off to college. The local school board members (farmers themselves) suspected that as a wheat farmer I had little to do during the non-growing season and urged me to consider teaching the children in the little school house a mile from the edge of our farm. There was one catch I was quick to announce. I lacked the proper credentials.

Not a problem, they said. The State Department of Education would issue an emergency teaching certificate to anyone who passed an examination currently held at the county seat. Emboldened by encouragement from Pat, my wife, I passed the exam and the following week was schoolmaster of eight children scattered over five grades.

Nowadays elementary school teachers teach several subjects to one class of pupils. Teachers in those ancient one-room schools taught all subjects to students in as many as eight grades, an impossible task surprisingly well done by many teachers, especially mine. Having neither training nor experience in teaching, I went about the tasks of teaching elementary school children in much the same way as did the teachers in the rural school I had attended.

As the younger children labored with reading, writing, spelling, and numbers – major effort for kids who spoke only German in their homes – I acquired overdue sympathy for my teachers. I gained new insight about the challenges of moving kids out of their preoccupation with recess and after-school fun and into the realm of abstractions. With the older pupils I quickly became immersed in the basic propositions of language, history, geography, arithmetic, and natural science. The exercise, as I recall, didn't particularly impress them. It was not stuff they necessarily needed in order to be farmers, an occupation they instinctively presumed to be their destiny. Several of them are still farmers.

There in those dark winter days in that North Dakota schoolhouse (there was no electricity to light the room) I began to ponder my preoccupation with farming. I became curious about the intellectual scenarios Pat described when reminiscing about her college days. She missed the creative opportunities and intellectual stimulation she experienced at college.

So after several years we left the farm – resolved to return someday – and at the age of twenty-seven I enrolled in college where I encountered my first professors. While becoming a professor was not my intention, it was the beginning of an unintentional drift into a delightful four-decade diversion into the domain of ideas. My grandfather was right. "Be a professor. It beats working for a living," he said.

Reluctant Readers

Among those who write books are professors who write textbooks. Textbooks are seldom, if ever, best sellers. But a good textbook is usually assured of some sales because it is the prerogative of professor-authors to place their titles on the list of required reading for their students. That may not necessarily insure their books will be read, however. The number of books purchased and the number of books read is quite likely not to be the same. This is particularly true of college textbooks.

There are books that probably don't have to be read and perhaps some that ought not to be read. Students seem to know instinctively which they are. Of course, the final defense – and one frequently employed by students against such books – is not to read them. By not reading, students avoid contending with thoughts of wasted time.

Should one want to discover which books should not be read there are but two options: read the book or find someone who has. The latter is not as easy as one might think and students may not have time for that.

Society, whether by design or default, has provided reluctant readers some recourse. There are persons whose business it is to write about the writing of others. That's called doing research. One hopes that these researchers will have read the writing about which they are writing. Reading this research requires a great measure of faith and the catch is that one must resort to reading anyway. One might as well read the writing about which these writers are writing.

The Bible is a book about which much has been written. And one learns quickly that it is much less confusing to read the Bible itself. In fact, the writer of Ecclesiastes anticipated this predicament when he wrote "of the making of books there is no end and much study is a weariness of the flesh." One wonders how so many students seem to know that.

There is another, although expensive, way to avoid reading and still find out which books should not be read. Go to college! There are persons there whose job it is to read books and then to tell others what the books are about. These people are called professors. The ones being told are called students. Professors make speeches called lectures in which they tell students what is written in the textbook (which all were required to purchase and after two weeks the whereabouts is uncertain). Of course, students can't really know how accurately the professor's comments reflect the contents of the textbook without resorting to reading, but most have more exciting things to do.

Early in my professorial career I noticed that the ability to read is not necessarily a college entrance prerequisite. Students who can read, but don't, have no particular advantage over those who can't. It requires some professorial experience to tell the difference. But by the time professors acquire that skill, most realize that it doesn't really matter. What matters most is that students get credit for the course. Only then will they return next term and pay some more tuition. And that is in the economic best interest of the professor.

There is another use for textbooks – one which is regularly exploited by experienced students and learned quickly by alert beginners. A stack of unread textbooks can function as a significant savings account, which becomes accessible about the time the students' funds are depleted. Usually around spring break. This typically happens when it becomes apparent to wakeful students that the textbook is, indeed, superfluous because the professor's lectures have been systematically divulging the book's contents and any need to read further no longer exists. The sale of "used books" yields a handsome sum just in time to finance spring-break activities, which generally don't include reading even though many students leave campus with good intentions and a backpack full of library books.

All of which confirms my belief that students are not dumb. Why read a book that probably should not have been written in the first place and quite likely is being revised anyway? Students should not be hassled about reading. Tuition being what it is, the price they pay for the privilege not to is high enough.

Perquisites Pertaining Thereto

The sun was coming up as we circled the airbase waiting for other bombers to gain altitude and join the formation, which then would make its way over the Alps and on to Germany. Our crew was captained by an irreverent, sometimes reckless, incredibly skilled, nineteen-year-old pilot from Washington. I was the eighteen-year-old tail gunner from Minnesota. The rest of the crew were twenty-something guys from West Virginia, New Jersey, New York, Colorado, California, Illinois, and Iowa.

Our mission that day was not typical – typical is a questionable adjective for battle. It was long. The conflict was intense. The losses were substantial and some heroes fell. I wasn't one of them for which I have been forever grateful.

Ours was a typical bomber crew, nothing unusual about any of us. We had trained together for several months before arriving in what was called the European Theater of War, a curious designation for a battleground, since no one was pretending. Only one of the guys had any college experience and, strangely, there was seldom any chatter about college as a postwar option. There were more pressing, immediate concerns.

When the battles were over in Europe, our crew was dismantled and I was shipped (military jargon for being sent) to the U.S.A. for additional training anticipating duty in the Pacific Theatre. (There's that word again.) Fortunately, that fracas ended before my training was complete. I was moved about the western states for several months, eventually discharged, and arrived home a few weeks before my twentieth birthday.

Congress decreed that all of the men and women who served in the conflict were entitled to a college education financed by the government: a perquisite from a grateful nation. It was called the GI Bill. I don't know whether any of my crew exploited the opportunity – I know that none of them are professors. The benefit was of minor interest to me. I was going to be a farmer and it hadn't yet occurred to me that *educated farmer* was not an oxymoron. Few of the farmers of my parents' generation had attended college. The only encouragement I received was from a devout aunt, who believed I should go to college and study to be a Lutheran minister. By the way, that thought was not affirmed by the local parish pastor. I set out to seek my fortune as a farmer.

Seven years later our farming enterprise was not developing the way we had hoped. After agonizing deliberation we decided to suspend this passion of mine and I would go to college – ironically, to become a preacher.

That's when I remembered the GI bill. And so along with applications to colleges, I registered my wish to be included in this perk and allow the taxpayers to fund my education. Nearly eight years had elapsed since the initiation of the program and most of the GIs had made their way through the universities. The Veterans Administration was anxious to close the books on this project and invited me to travel to the nearest office to discuss the matter. I was subjected to several aptitude tests and an interview with a government psychologist. It was the decision of these examiners that it would be in everybody's best interest if I would stay on the farm. I think it was the government's best interest about which they were most concerned. That was strange, however, inasmuch as the government was spending a lot of money subsidizing marginal farmers like me.

Typically, the government was not inclined to explain or justify the conclusion. They probably mistook the enthusiasm with which I described what I had been doing as ambivalence about leaving the farm and weren't ready to risk the government's money (some of which was mine) sending someone who looked and talked too much like a farmer away to college. I tell myself that surely they didn't question my aptitude for college. They must have failed to recognize that my fascination with farming was greater in the abstract than it was in reality.

"Stay on the farm," they said. "That's where you belong." More than a denial of funding, their decision felt like an indictment of my intellectual aptitude. But I had learned that government workers were wrong as often as they were right. There was, therefore, a fifty per cent chance that I would succeed. Despite being denied this GI perk, we embarked on what was to become a ten-year sojourn in the realm of "book learning," heretofore considered superfluous for farmers. I was innocently on the road to professordom.

A few years into my pursuit of knowledge, the Russians sent Sputnik into orbit. Feeling left behind, Congress passed The National Defense Education Act (NDEA). Alarmed by what they had considered deficiencies in the education of scientists, they offered financial support for individuals who would acquire Ph.D. degrees and commit to teaching science at the nation's colleges and universities.

In the meantime, although minimally prepared I had accepted a serendipitous invitation to teach biology at a California university. Encountering students brighter than I quickly convinced me that the professoriate could be my true destiny only if I retreated to some sanctuary of higher learning. My pursuit of wisdom was about to become a means to an end.

It is remarkable how much more astute the government assessors of aptitude had become since my skirmish with them about the GI bill. They readily endorsed my application for a NDEA fellowship – a bonus that vindicated our decision not to stay on the farm – and expedited my excursion through the maze of doctoral studies at the University of Yores. I was solemnly awarded not only the Ph.D. degree "with all the rights and privileges pertaining thereto" but a faculty position in which to pursue it all. I was now a professor strangely struggling with an urge to go back to the farm and ponder it all.

A Manner of Speaking

When I walked into my very first college class, the students mistook me for the professor. It was a legitimate mistake. I was nearly thirty years old, graying prematurely and with a look of concern on my face that the other first-year students mistakenly assumed to be in their interest. Momentarily, I was startled by the thought that these students had been in contact with my long-deceased grandfather. But it soon became apparent to them that I was not the professor. That I didn't immediately begin to talk seems to have been their first clue.

Unfortunately, they had already learned that it was the professor's task to talk and it was theirs was to listen. They were right. Lecturing, a professor's self-assigned primary activity, involves standing before an audience of students and telling them what their reading assignment should have told them.

A good professor doesn't waste time not talking. A professor's livelihood is dependent on opportunities to talk. One has only to enter a classroom to discover that professors believe it is their prerogative to talk and that they do a lot of it, much of it to themselves. The significance (or insignificance) of what they are talking about is not always apparent to the students. And the number of them listening is not necessarily an indication either. Whether anyone listens or not, it is the act of talking that makes one a professor.

Some professors instinctively suppose that every proposition falls within their intellectual niche and that they are obliged to talk about it. (That's most obvious at faculty meetings.) It was in college where I was surprised to discover that professors think it is incumbent upon them to talk, especially when no one else is. It is remarkable how uncomfortable professors are with silence and how readily they attempt to improve upon it. Frequently, they are too busy talking to notice that some people aren't. Too slowly I realized that my silent attempts to think of something to say were taken as signals that I had nothing to say. Unwittingly, I presented my colleagues with innumerable opportunities to talk.

One doesn't need to be around professors long to notice that there is a lot of sameness about what a given professor says about everything. This is especially true of full professors. Full professors are those who know a lot more than anyone else about some little thing, which eventually leaves them little to talk about. Their only recourse is to invent new ways to say the same old thing. The number of titles assigned to the same course (or book) is amazing.

Professors are designated as professors of something, e.g., Professor of Biology, which implies that they have something about which to talk. There are professors of art, biology, chemistry, geography, history, etcetera – all the traditional compartments of academe. And because there are so many people who aspire to be professors, new categories of things about which to profess have been invented. There are professors of agribusiness, biomedical ethics, conflict resolution, dysteleological philosophy, ecclesiastical psychology, gender studies, and zymurgy. It is not uncommon for a professor of one of these fragments of knowledge to become tenured. Then students and society are stuck with another set of jargon with which to clutter their minds and muddle their thinking. But that's the stuff of which professors' jobs are made.

Inasmuch as professors have been ordained to talk and have acquired something to talk about, they need someone to talk to. In fact, the livelihood of professors depends upon the willingness of people (usually young people) to subject themselves to the chatter of professors. Society in its goodness proclaimed that institutions should be created to provide opportunities for its young folks to sit at the feet of professors and become informed and responsible citizens. In doing so our culture has, quite inadvertently, guaranteed not only that young people learn how to sit at the feet of professors but also secured a source of spectators to whom professors are paid to speak.

Much of what is professed can be found in books or papers. In fact, many professors transpose their lectures into print. Considering the incentives of the game, it is in their professional best interest to do so. But why students prefer to sit in classrooms with hundreds of their peers listening to a professor prattle on about what is printed in the book he or she has written (rather than read the stuff themselves) continues to puzzle me. This disposition of students does, indeed, sustain the economic well being of professors, inasmuch as it provides them with activity for which to get paid while they are inventing new ideas or another way to talk about old ones. The presence of students inadvertently encourages them to keep talking.

Learning to be a professor does require one to become skilled at talking until one has thought of something to say, hereby retaining the opportunity to continue. This is most useful when a student has asked a question. It is imperative that the professor master the skill of reclaiming the podium when having been interrupted by an alert student who did, indeed, read the professor's treatise.

When professors tire of classroom professing – no longer willing to compete with conversations among students about more interesting things – many retire to Centers for Advanced Thinking to become society's experts on anything and everything. They jealously reserve their professorial prerogative to talk and readily accept all invitations offered by TV talk show hosts to do so. No longer required to prepare 50-minute lectures they are content to deliver their expertise in 20-second sound bites, frequently at the same time another authority is expertizing from a contrary perspective.

Guarding expertise is an important dimension of the academy but does not justify talking at the same time as others who had assumed it was their turn. Waiting one's turn, however, is not easy for professors bursting with information and opinion.

Meeting of the Minds

Of all the peripheral activities in which we professors participate, none is more central to our collective identity than the faculty meeting. And none is more fun than these meetings of the minds. Being a professor with some sense of responsibility I have attended more faculty meetings than I care to admit. To observe these rituals is to be both amused and confused and left in a state of disbelief that they actually do happen.

As individuals, professors are quite tolerable – most are even delightful. While I didn't always like what some of them said, I have never met a professor I didn't like. But a roomful of professors is an enigma. It is remarkable how quickly a faculty meeting can transform a group of even the wisest of us into a bunch of bumbling boondogglers. On the other hand, one should not be surprised, inasmuch as each professor is by definition an expert with a different notion about how the world – and subsequently the college – should work and presumes that both the world and the college want to know about it. No matter what the agenda item, a debate inevitably ensues and the usual result is another demonstration of professors' proclivity to prioritize the peripheral. I know. I have participated often enough to be rated among the best – or the worst.

I have concluded that when the assignments of this world were made there were some tasks not given to professors. Chief among them is to agree. One of my favorite deans once said that he never had any difficulty identifying professors. "They are the one's who always think otherwise," he said. It should be no surprise that consensus is difficult to achieve when some professors think the world is real, some think that it is not, and some don't even think – not at all unacceptable at faculty meetings.

In retrospect, I think it is quite ambitious to expect consensus to emerge in a group which includes: mathematicians who think reality is an equation, literature profs who think it's a story, musicians who think it's sound, dramatists who think it's a play, coaches who think it's a game, physicists who think it's energy, chemists who think it's matter, theologians who think it's non-material, philosophers who think it's immaterial, sociologists who think it doesn't matter, and biologists who *know* it is all of that. Yet attempting accord is a challenge the faculty eagerly accepts. That we keep trying continues to amaze me.

There are at faculty meetings, nevertheless, two occasions on which we professors readily agree. The proposition that no one (especially those at the meeting) is being paid what he or she is worth invariably receives unanimous support.

The other is a loose, unwritten but agreed upon, set of ideals about what qualifies one to be a faculty leader. Acceptable leaders cannot be persons who think too much, nor should they be persons who don't think at all. Most acceptable are those whose thoughts are relatively harmless. I do take some small comfort in having been judged insufficiently incompetent to be an acceptable leader. I learned to enjoy being a follower. A follower seldom has to apologize.

A faculty meeting's most redeeming feature is its humor. Having learned early not to take either myself or my colleagues too seriously, it was my fondness for the funniness of faculty meetings that lured my attendance. A verbatim account of what is spoken by professors for the record during faculty meetings is really quite amusing. The meeting is not over until everything that could be said about anything is said by everyone. Every professor feels obliged to comment – often with brilliant verbigeration and from his or her professional perspective, of course.

Some of it is meant to be comedic; much of it is not. Some of it is funny simply because it has little to do with the issue in question. Some of it is wit intended primarily to display talent or to effectively distract from the issue in question. By the time the laughter subsides, most have lost sight of the action before the house, which probably was an administrative matter anyway.

What happens at a faculty meeting may affect the participants, but it can also make a difference for those who didn't come. It is tempting to admire those few professors who have sense enough to stay away. Some do, indeed, realize that their presence won't really improve the meeting and should be commended for that.

But I think staying away is unkind. Absenting oneself leaves the impression that what one's colleagues are doing there is unimportant. While that may be true, to hurt someone with the truth is a most unkind thing to do and cannot be overlooked in deliberations about tenure.

Probably in some mysterious yet-to-be-understood way, faculty meetings may, indeed, serve some useful function. However, the most I have come to expect is to hear some creative new way to continue doing the same old thing.

Deans, Deaning & Deanlets

Among life's minor annoyances are encounters with people who know better. Such engagements are frequent in the lives of professors. In the academic arena there are actually persons whose officially designated function is to know better and whose prerogative it is to say so: they are called deans. Sometimes they are called provosts, but usually that name is reserved for deans for whom the university has no further use.

Professors are experts and experts by definition must be right. Defending expertise is costly and precludes being wrong. However, it is in a professor's best interest not to push that advantage in the inevitable discord with deans about additional staff, space, classes, and funds. Young professors must learn how to circumvent the dean. Tenured profs can wait them out.

If a professor wishes to maintain a modicum of self-esteem, he or she must quickly learn how to manage deans. It is not a skill that comes easily and can only be learned by doing it. Novice professors should proceed with caution. In encounters with the dean they should avoid leaving the impression they think the dean is wrong. They must learn the distinction between knowing better and the dean's prerogative to be wrong. The trek to tenure is smoother for rookie professors who realize that having a job is more expeditious than being right.

Like professors, most deans take themselves too seriously. What they don't take seriously enough, however, are the risks inherent in taking themselves too seriously. With that mentality it is difficult for them to stay out of the way. Isn't it interesting how deans who are expected to know everything get in the way of professors who do?

The whimsy that deans are well enough informed in all disciplines to know what is best for any of them is probably sustained by the common practice of selecting deans from departments of philosophy or education, disciplines which have no content that is exclusively their own. Thus, deans are not burdened by details with which professors must contend. (What biology professor has not been annoyed by the dean's failure to recognize the distinction between DNA and TBA?)

I suppose in some obscure way deans serve some useful purpose. But I must confess that after thirty years at Migh College I don't have a clear notion about what that is. It has been said that the role of the college president is to make speeches. The faculty's role is to think. And the dean's role is to keep the faculty from making speeches and the president from thinking. I could never see any great risk in faculty persons giving speeches or from the president thinking. Thinking presidents are a good thing and some of them may welcome a little respite from speaking, inasmuch as they frequently have more opportunities to talk than they have things to talk about. And it could be, while making speeches, professors might realize they don't have all that much to say. However, I can see how all this may eliminate the need for deans.

When I reminisce about deans who have known me I recall some of them making it obvious that anyone could be the dean, while others just as effectively demonstrated that deans are not really necessary. The most common response to the question of why we need deans is: "Well, somebody has to do it." That response invariably comes from the deans and their associates, affectionately known here at Migh College as deanlets.

Actually, Migh College experimented with not having an official dean. The traditional activities of that office were scattered among several faculty members. The experiment failed because no acceptable title was found for the professors to whom these deaning tasks were assigned. I suggested deanlets, but that was rejected as impudent. Some profs saw a parallel between deans and deanlets and ducks and ducklings and with masterful metaphoric skill argued that one could not have ducklings if there were no duck.

During my tenure at Migh College, the average tenancy of deans was 3.76 years. That's not only about the time it takes deans to tire of always being wrong, it is also the time it takes them to realize nobody is listening. A veteran dean-watcher learns quickly to exploit that turnover. An ideal time to propose a change in staff, funding, or curriculum is the moment an incumbent dean realizes that his or her deanship is doomed. The request will be lost in the stack of paper work that accumulates while the dean is away interviewing for the next vacant college presidency. Not having been officially denied, the proposed change can be initiated – only to be discovered by the new dean about the time he or she realizes that the notion professors can be managed is a myth.

For the most part deans in my experience were intelligent folks. But deaning is an impossible task. The faculty dissenters doom any honest effort to manage a faculty. It makes me wonder why so many professors yearn to be deans. Some might innocently attach prestige to the assignment, while others see it as the only hope for an increase in income. I suspect some naiveté exists in the minds of would-be deans, notably the notion that anyone (especially oneself) could do a better job than the incumbent. I confess thinking that.

I think profs who aspire to become the dean haven't been paying attention to the paradox of successful deaning, which is that one has to be intelligent enough to do it but also unwise enough to think it's necessary.

Awakened to the realization that a new dean has arrived, the professor's first step in dean management is to encourage him or her to begin thinking that he or she is a potential candidate for the next available college presidency. With all the modesty I can muster, I submit it was not my fault that anyone became the dean. However, I did sense a responsibility to ease their disquiet about having to leave, which occasionally required me to make my way to the inner office to affirm their decision to do so. I submit as evidence of my dean-watching status a comment by a younger colleague to whom I had announced that I was on my way to the dean's office. "Why?" he asked, "What's he done now?"

Fabrication

Distracted during the commencement address by construction machinery across the street, I began recounting the number of similar rituals I had endured. In my reverie I realized that fifteen years had gone by since I had spent the summer months following commencement exercises doing something other than attending summer school, either as a student or teacher. Right then I resolved to spend the impending summer doing something more concrete.

The next day I signed on as a carpenter with a contractor friend. I wanted to challenge my grandfather's suspicion that professors are incapable of anything but trafficking in ideas. Also, I yearned for the satisfaction of standing back at the end of an exhausting day and actually seeing what I had accomplished, a rare experience in the daily routine of professing. I was eager to exploit latent skills I acquired in high school shop courses in which my immigrant parents insisted I enroll — crafts honed while building barns with my carpenter father.

We, the crew and I, built three houses that summer. It was not the clean inside work my grandfather promised would be mine if I became a professor. It was hard work and there was some heavy lifting, but it produced the good-feeling kind of tiredness that I remembered from my college days in construction and earlier on the farm. Best of all, I could stand back at day's end and see what I had accomplished.

During my summer sojourn in the real world of concrete, lumber, sand, wire, and pipe I met artisans delightfully different from my professor friends. While enormously skilled in their chosen crafts, their notions about politics, money, sex, and religion were often unexamined and stated in language lacking the jargon so eloquently employed by my professional ideologues. Unlike professors, they were quite content to let the positions of others go unchallenged. After all, their merit rested on how well they manufactured houses not on their skill in massaging abstractions. Occasionally I was invited to challenge or buttress an argument not because they had any investment in the position but, as they confessed, to observe a professor at work.

My carpenter friends, while not formally educated, were not unintelligent guys. Most had never encountered professors with Ph.D. degrees and they had no notions about advanced degrees except to slyly suggest that it meant one had stayed in college too long. While not indifferent to my academic credentials, they ascribed little significance to them. They delighted in quoting an older co-worker with only a second grade education, who was a master at improvisation in all the building trades. When asked how he knew to do all those things he would say, "When you ain't educated, you have to use your head."

As the summer moved on, the novelty of an authentic professor doing their kind of work began to diminish; still they delighted in introducing me as The Professor to inspectors, truck drivers or workers from the other trades. "The Professor will help you," they would say, conjuring in me memories of my grandfather. The usual response of these workers was to assume "professor" was a comment about my demeanor, not my actual occupation. The suspicion that professors can't do anything else may, indeed, be as prevalent as my grandfather wanted to believe.

From the carpenters with whom I worked I learned again to frame walls, cut rafters, build trusses, set windows, hang doors, and build forms for concrete structures. I began to think my parents were right after all. Maybe I was, indeed, intended to follow in my immigrant father's vocation.

At my real professorial work I often measured the progress of my students by the extent to which they had begun to think as biologists, i.e., like I do. Who knows what carpenters think about, but I began to think – like I suspect carpenters think – that building real things in the real world has merit, no less commendable or virtuous than building ideas or shaping the thinking of young people.

Rarely while professing did I entertain doubts about my competence fabricating abstractions and maneuvering students through the maze, and hardly ever was I unhappy doing so. But that summer I realized I could be as content constructing houses as I was fabricating ideas. In fact, the summer was the beginning of some private, professional dissonance which I later managed by doing both. In subsequent summers I designed and literally built several houses. My father would have been proud. I never again attended summer school.

Four-year-old Joey summed up my season of reprieve late that summer. He frequently tagged along with his father on inspection tours assessing the progress of their new house. His father, a former student of mine, had introduced me to the child as Professor. My fellow craftsmen (so that they could stay at their work) assigned to me the task of attending to visitors at the site. They enjoyed saying, "The Professor will help you." Consequently, I had had several conversations with Joey.

On one occasion he silently watched me on my knees leveling sand in the bottom of a form I had built for a concrete patio. Later, back in the house he was asked if he knew what the professor was doing. "He's playing in his sandbox by the back door," was his unhesitant reply. He was right. Not only was it fun, it was delightfully devoid of intellectual ostentation.

I had not thought of my summer school absenteeism as frivolity. But I suspected the deans might have. "One does not build an impressive resume pursuing frivolous non-academic digressions," the memo said. I was reminded that professors when not in the classroom are expected to keep busy easing back the edges of the unknown or rearranging the known into novel, historical scenarios. I knew that. But I had commenced this caper in carpentry deliberately not blind to the professional consequences. In fact, they became quite clear the moment I took up my hammer and saw.

The Meritocracy

With the possible exception of professors themselves, everybody harbors suspicions that we professors are a peculiar bunch. Four decades in academia observing professors has persuaded me that, as a group, we are more ordinary than most of us care to admit. We live and work, however, in a context where the rhetoric of distinction and elitism causes us to think of ourselves as anything but ordinary. Notions of excellence and brilliance are prattled about until everyone believes there actually is an objective scale of merit – with the brightest on top and lesser lights on lower levels all the way to the bottom.

Unfortunately, a lot of creativity and intellectual energy is directed away from the teaching function of colleges and universities by the scramble for status on this scale of distinction. Should not some merit accrue to those who are not driven by that aspect of the incentive structures and prefer to exploit their intellectual creativity and energy in encounters with students?

Such activity, however, is perilous for a professor aspiring for recognition and gains one little affirmation from the meritocracy, while prestige accrues automatically to scholarly achievements that enhance the reputation and economic well being of the stars – and the university. It seems to me, the farther these meritocrats get from the excitement of youthful curiosity and deeper into the business of trafficking in ideas for their own sake, less of what they do is of much benefit to undergraduate students. The pursuit of prestige lessens their contact with young people.

The professors under whose tutelage I studied, as well as many of those with whom I worked, were overall a delightful, diverse, not-infrequently perverse bunch. Not naturally bent towards modesty I have been known to imply, somewhat audaciously perhaps, that my becoming an intellectual was something I managed in spite of my professors. (An astute reader will recognize the two assumptions in that avowal.) I will acknowledge that much, if not all, of the intrigue I have for ideas can be credited to about a dozen of my undergraduate professors. In my judgment they were real scholars, passionate in allegiance to their ideological niches, competent in argument and articulation, expansively aware of competing or contrary themes, contagiously fascinated with well-fabricated ideas, and unapologetically dedicated to the intellectual development of beginning college students.

If the definition of scholar is confined to those who write a lot of papers or books, the meritocracy would not necessarily recognize my professors as such. But they were as brilliant as any of the scholar-celebrities sequestered in think tank conglomerates like *The Center for This, The*

Institute for That, The Foundation for The Other Thing, or *The Council on Advanced Thinking about Everything* whose scholarly pursuits have little impact on inquisitive young people. It falls to lower-rung, ordinary profs to sort through all the esoterica generated by these intellectual heavy-weights to ascertain what, if any of it, is significant to undergraduates endeavoring to understand and find their place in the world.

I would be naive to dismiss the activity of these scholarly elite as trivial. In the great scheme of human thought they fuel the economy of ideas which preserves the essence of our culture. Few there are who delight more than I in rummaging through these manipulations of our culture's colossal collection of words and ideas. Nevertheless, I reserve the right to judge some of them nonsense and to argue much of it falls outside the domain of education as it is perceived by ordinary folks and especially parents who struggle to pay $20,000 a year to educate each of their children.

The alleged intellectual superiority of a university faculty by the presence of an internationally reputed star on its faculty roster is often immodestly proffered as an invaluable benefit for undergraduate scholars. Indeed, these top-rung scholars do have immense public relations and fund-raising worth, but very little of the funds (or ideas) are diverted downward to the actual task of educating the undergraduates. The educational enterprise is not, to borrow a phrase, a trickle-down economy.

One's rung on the academic ladder is of little significance outside the academic hierarchy. It is the significance attributed to status by the system within the academy that sustains the hierarchy. To avoid being taken hostage by this rhetoric of brilliance and distinction demands more diligence than a lot of beginning professors can muster. And being denied promotion doesn't make it any easier. I know, I've been there. It really becomes difficult if one harbors thoughts of inferiority implied by the dogma of the meritocracy. The message is relentless: genius in the daily grind with first-year students doesn't measure up to one bit of professional writing no matter how trivial.

One more meticulous manipulation of minutiae about old ideas fails to impress me nearly as much as the prof who stayed late to tutor a curious but confused student. The point of all this is to argue that there should be a place in the system for the recognition of a few ordinary professors, whose unapologetic dedication to scholarly teaching of young people is unencumbered by demands to demonstrate scholarship in the one-dimensional incentive of the meritocracy. But there are no high-level rungs on the ladder for that. And the risk of writing too much about it could be perceived as an apology from the lower rungs.

Rank Ritualism

My dictionary lists three uses of the word *rank*. Used as a noun, *rank* may indicate relative position in a scale of dignity as in a row of objects or persons lined up in a row, i.e., side by side. The latter meaning has little application in the protocol of professors. We function in a meritocracy ingrained with the belief that there are clear measures of distinction. We prefer to line up in front of the ones behind us. The verb *to rank* means to place in or assign to a position. Therefore, one who has been ranked has been put in his or her place. The adjective *rank* may be employed pejoratively, as in "rank ritualism." All three of these words come to mind when I am reminded of my participation in the professorial pecking order.

There are rituals in professorial protocol that may cause us to become rankled about rank or about having been ranked. One occasion is when we professors line up adorned in colorful regalia to march into an arena for convocation or commencement ceremonies. I know of no faculty in which there are fewer notions about how the professoriate should be ordered in an academic procession than there are professors participating. There is a somewhat tattered tradition that insists Professors march ahead of Associate Professors who, in turn, march ahead of Assistant Professors. (I think it is we professors who insist, but the tradition is blamed.) Within the ranks it also has been traditional for persons to be ordered by longevity in rank. Therefore, in order to stay in line (which is important to professors) they have to remember not only who is better than they but also who is older. In many institutions the tradition has been allowed to erode. Perhaps administrators grew weary of wrangling over rank. But the territoriality persists and the manifestations are interesting to behold.

In our profession, like all others, it is expedient for one to know one's place. When one's actual place and one's preferred place are in tension, one must resort to flattery. Bright young professors learn quickly that asking, "May I march behind you?" invariably gets a positive response. However, choosing the right person to ask can be a bit tricky. An alternative is to hide in the hallway or bushes and step into one's rightful place in the line as it passes, avoiding any argument at the moment. I don't recommend that. It risks rankling ranking persons and that could provoke unpleasant post-parade admonishments.

On occasion I would permit my peers to march ahead of me. Never did any of them challenge my right to be at the end of the line. It gave them an uncommon chance to be ahead of me and that made them feel good. (Is it not written somewhere that "the last shall be first"?) I know professors who attempt to leave the impression that they are above all this nonsense by staying away. I didn't ever do that. It's hard to be noticed when you aren't there.

In daily campus affairs few professors are noticeable. Teaching assistants are doing their work. But in public events where somebody may be watching – the board of trustees, the dean, or tuition paying parents – visibility is important. To enhance conspicuity professors resort to costuming for the occasion. This tradition shows no sign of abatement and invites professors to participate without restraint.

One undeniable perquisite of academic achievement is the freedom to attire oneself in resplendent regalia. Convention permits a novice to be clad as colorfully as a veteran. Ostentatious black robes are worn with modesty suggesting oneness with the profession, while one's identity is boldly reclaimed with color and adornments appropriate to one's university, degree, and guild. This is rank ritualism of the highest degree.

Theologians are most visible, readily identified by red – their self-assigned color. They initiated the tradition, which gave them first choice. Blazes of yellow mark the scientists. (I love my brilliant yellow chevrons.) Faded and pale blue are appropriate for education professors and philosophers, respectively. Other crafts have their adopted colors too, but few (other than those who wear them) are impressed.

I know of no profession other than the clergy that parades its credentials with quite the same immodesty. Although public patronage of this pageantry varies, professors have no plans to abandon the practice. Certainly we professors must be allowed some way of bringing a little order and color to our lives.

The Perils of Peerlessness

A significant privilege enjoyed by professors is evaluation by their peers. The practice is fair enough except for those few persons who have no peers because they are so exceptional at what they are doing, something that defies both evaluation and understanding. Fortunately, few professors suffer from that kind of peerlessness. It is difficult to be without peer on the lower rungs of the academic meritocracy.

It is possible and, indeed, quite probable that some professors have few or no peers because nobody likes them. That circumstance, however, is not unique to professors. There are people who manage to alienate others regardless of where they work. But that is not the sort of peerlessness of which I write. There are persons who are so far ahead of the contenders that the crowd has lost sight of them or are so far behind that their contention doesn't matter. One can be without peer at either extreme. I have had colleagues in both categories.

As for my place among peers, I managed a modicum of scholarly achievement, which was evaluated by my departmental peerage. I was awarded tenure and the rank of full professor, which I accepted with appropriate humility. My experience in peerlessness, however, was of a different sort. I avoided ardent allegiance to any single ideology about the way the world works. It was not that I was unable to choose. My decision not to endorse any single scenario about the nature and meaning of existence was deliberate, and I came to accept the consequent loss of peers. I think my grandfather would have been proud of me. He would say, "Always carry a ladder when you are digging holes."

To insist that the world functions only according to rules fashioned by one's favorite paradigm is intellectual self-deprivation of the saddest kind. Unfortunately, to achieve distinction in the ranks of intellectuals one must be devoted to making the world fit the proscriptions of one's guild. I was not inclined to do that, nor am I any longer apologetic for my inability to muster the required fealty to do so.

Rather, I chose to ignore the artificial perimeters of ideological turfdoms and became comfortable wandering about paradigms other than the one in which I had been licensed. I was particularly intrigued by the reputed irreconcilability of religious and scientific schemes. I imagined myself a biologian. (My computer's spell check rejected *biologian* – change to *bologna* it suggested.) I found rummaging through the tenets of theologians to be a fascinating diversion, although one not destined to enhance the professional reputation of a reluctant reductionist molecular biologist.

While this predilection probably precluded my becoming an expert in either discipline, it did allow me to wonder if there might be another way – a question experts cannot risk asking themselves. I have not encountered many professors, their alleged allegiance to liberal education notwithstanding, who are comfortable beyond the periphery of their favorite paradigms. To wander too far beyond the boundaries of one's discipline is to find oneself without peers. And to be found peerless is not without peril, especially at promotion time. The freedom to indulge in a little intellectual adventurism, however, is well worth the risk.

Death by Degree

A peril worse than peerlessness threatens the young, unsuspecting, would-be professor. I am always surprised when asked if I'm engaged in a hazardous profession. This usually occurs when I'm donating blood or buying insurance, both of which are useful things for professors to do. My instinctive reply and that of most of my professor friends is, "Of course not." But all occupations have perils and none are quite as subtle as those that befall us as self-proclaimed custodians of culture's repository of abstractions.

The realization that there are occupational dangers to be avoided in this business does not readily occur to beginners and, sadly, in many cases not at all. While it is unlikely that a professor will incur bodily injury defending ideological high ground, death by degree on the other hand is not uncommon. Beginners are the most vulnerable.

Aspiring professors ought to know about the snares awaiting them that could hobble the rest of their intellectual lives. Common decency should require mentors of would-be professors to warn them of this impending danger, but such caution is usually not included in the rites of passage. The neglect may be intentional, which would be most unkind. But I am suspicious that many mentors may not have avoided this most perilous pitfall themselves, which is to move beyond the point at which their ideological constructs become confused with the real world.

It is inconceivable that thinking people would intentionally embrace barriers that preclude their thinking otherwise. Yet this trap seems unavoidable and persists as the major hazard confronting would-be professors pursuing the Ph.D. To have one's way of looking at the world turned to stone by the very process with which one learns about the world seems to me most unfortunate. Yet what neophyte Ph.D. doesn't naively display the intellectual blinders imposed on him or her by the specialization required in the pursuit of the degree.

Although acquiring a Ph.D. is seen as a mark of distinction (especially by those who have one), it is a task that requires as much temerity as it does intelligence. Fortunately, it is not an incurable condition, but it does take time to recover from a Ph.D. The brighter novices eventually recognize that the temple of truth to which they have been invited to carry their intellectual sacrifices exists mostly in the imagination of the faithful. In the meantime, having nothing else to say many young professors subject their students and colleagues to innumerable renditions of the same theme. It is amazing how many titles the same lecture can have.

I believe their recovery would be expedited if all new professors were to be constrained from mentioning their dissertations until they have been in the business long enough to realize the insignificance of them. Perhaps by then they will have developed some immunity to further impairment of their intellectual well being. After all, who cares about *Immunoelectrophoretic Comparisons of the Ontogeny of Liver Antigens in Avian Species?*

Academic Circles

Academic circles, a metaphor frequently employed in the literature of the academy, traditionally connotes the intellectual and political environment in which professors run around. The simile is so deeply embedded in academic thinking that very little of professorial routine escapes metaphoric abuse.

Consider the concentric strata into which the incentives of the academy with its premium on publication effectively centrifuges the reputed intellectual heavyweights to the outer circles of scholarly merit. The idiom is also said to characterize the circular logic frequently observed in scholarly debate or the cyclic nature of the academic year. Some professors see academic circles in the hoops through which they must jump for advancement, but I think that is pushing the analogy too far. Although, it may be the perfect allusion to the run-around minor professors receive from the dean or threatened senior professors guarding the road to promotion and tenure. After all, it is a common experience for professors to realize they are right back where they started from.

Whatever meaning one attaches to the idiom, there is indeed a lot of circularity in the everyday activities of professors. It is fascinating to observe the various angles from which they approach a problem. Inasmuch as there are no absolute right angles in academia, a wise professor will avoid taking a problem straight on. A stratagem successfully employed by English professors to rationalize additional departmental staff is to argue that each different spin Shakespeare scholars put on the same comedy circumspectly requires an additional professor. Not always obvious to the dean, this caper does provide employment opportunities for English majors and no doubt accounts for the disproportionate number of English professors on many faculties. But since earth spins only in one direction, physics profs are unfairly limited in the spin they may put on their courses, thereby maintaining the prevailing five-to-one ratio of English and Physics professors in most universities.

My first encounters with literal academic circles occurred when I was left to dismantle the rings of chairs into which sociologists and education professors had arranged my classroom. The arrangement allowed their students to sit facing each other and contribute their innocence to the con-fabulation, thereby absolving the professors of the task of preparing a lecture. Having only one-dimensional con-structs unencumbered with equations or the need for black-boards, sociology readily lends itself to circular discussions.

Then there is theatre-in-the-round, which actually makes sense as any attempt to portray life should be viewed from all angles. Ecologists in their clamor for environmental responsibility taught us about the cyclic processes of nature and the phenomenon of recycling – an idea not necessarily foreign to professors, who for generations have been recycling ideas, lectures, and tests and may now claim legitimacy for the practice.

I became so attuned to circular thought that when I began creating house plans (building houses had become a rewarding extracurricular activity) I started to envision circular floor plans. After a couple of houses I actually did design and build a twelve-sided, essentially round house. We have been living courageously in-the-round ever since.

We have become accustomed to the never-ending jokes about the rotunda, spiral staircase and orbital hallway in our dodecagonal floor plan. Colleagues practiced in circular logic are quick to notice the scarcity of corners in which to get trapped. Those who eschew direct approaches to difficult decisions seem to appreciate the unusual angles necessitated by the circular perimeter. Others see our plan as the optimal design for the turnabouts of administrative rotation.

When questioned about what motivated us to create our house-in-the-round, it seldom occurs to me that the all-encompassing nature of academia may have been the inspiration. It could be that all this palaver about academic circles may be *much ado about nothing.*" I just wanted to do something contrary, an ambition that circumscribes the thinking of most professors with time on their hands.

Managed Mussiness

My grandfather often said, "It's easy to spot a professor in a crowd except perhaps in a crowd of professors." I, too, have noticed that at a meeting of professors everyone looks alike. And it doesn't matter which group of professors is meeting. It is the not so subtle sameness in their attempts to be different that betrays them. They all end up looking like professors.

I would like to believe the dress of professors is a carefully studied aptitude. It takes a great deal of thought to appear as if one had given no thought to one's attire. But I don't think professors think that much about it. Scholarly attire is the one aspect of the professorial phenomenon that defies analysis – it seems to just happen. However, inasmuch as it's largely academic, it probably doesn't matter.

While it's possible that some professors intend their attire to make a statement, any correlation between a professor's attire and his or her academic niche is not readily discernable – except perhaps the heavy untied boots favored by female field-biologists. Still, there may be some clues in scholarly habit. Some professors' thoughts are as garbled as their garb, while the pieced-together apparel of others seems to match the eclectic logic of their arguments.

Does anyone know how mismatched buttonholes or unmatched socks relate to the collision of fact and fiction? Or what an inside-out sweater reveals about the hidden underside of a favorite ideological façade? Do the white coats of biologists really, as it has been claimed, symbolize the purity of their convictions? Disallowed in chem labs, bare feet and sandals are safe in the halls of literature where spillover seldom endangers either the feet or the minds of others.

Apart from business professors, dressed in suits and ties to demonstrate to their students the fashions of professionals who work for money, sartorial splendor is seldom seen in the ranks of professors. For a time sweats and warm-up garments (favored by phys-ed profs to display devotion to their craft) escaped to the halls of academe, but the fashion didn't catch on beyond the gym. Hooded sweat shirts (unlike hooded robes) were rejected outright by religion profs as failing to convey the proper solemnity expected of theologians.

Judging from the appearance of some of my colleagues, I don't think I ever looked much like a professor. I could never master the mussiness that attends the attire of many professors, especially philosophers and sociologists. (They are the masters of muddle, both ideologically and sartorially.)

My inability to look like a professor was not especially burdensome. Subconsciously, I may have attempted to cloak my professorial identity by disguising myself as a farmer. Now that I think about it, my grandfather tried not to look like a farmer. He dressed like a professor. He wore a not-so-neatly trimmed beard, which at that time was not common among farmers. I thought it gave him an aura of wisdom. Like most real professors, he thought so too. Ever wonder why so many professors wear beards? I wish I knew. I don't recall ever seeing a beard that made its bearer a better professor. If beards did, indeed, have that effect, it would be the only real advantage men would have over women professors.

Growing a beard didn't work for me. My wife told me it made me look short, fat, and old – not the affirmation I had hoped for. Any one of those was sufficient to cause me to re-evaluate the potency of my modest goatee. So I resigned myself to being a professor who looked like a farmer.

I adopted my dress code in graduate school at the University of Yores where everyone, students and professors alike, thought they were cowboys. Denim and boots were thought to make it so. Having at one time been a real cowboy the attire was natural for me. You have no idea how much fun it was being a professor who looked like a farmer. My colleagues tended to take me less seriously and – once I got used to it – it was delightfully freeing.

Over four decades in the profession I have observed a definite decline in the dignity of professorial dress. Whether this was by design or default is difficult to determine.

If by default, I wonder whose fault it was. I have concluded that students have been the leaders in the descent. Many of the student fashions are intended to display attitudes — which now that I think about it is probably also true of professors' sartorial statements. But why are the students so much better at it? Perhaps they are not constrained by delusions of distinction. Compelled by the need to look like all the others, students don't have to spend much thought on what to wear. They just look around at their peers.

Actually, I doubt that the attire of students or professors has much effect on either teaching or learning. My former students have perpetrated the legend that on test days I invariably appeared in the classroom attired in black — to deepen the doomsday emotion they were already experiencing, they contend. While I am inclined to argue that is largely fabrication, it's nice to think I was noticed. Perhaps that is what professorial attire is all about.

 # Believe It

When at the age of twenty-seven I left the farm to go to college, it was not my intention to become a professor. Driving a tractor (something a wheat farmer does a lot) is not necessarily mindless activity, but it does afford one countless hours of contemplation. As I harrowed the ground I became more and more curious about what makes the world and all the people on it go around. I had been raised to believe that God had something to do with that and was led to think that preachers knew the most about God. So when I eventually left the fields to go to college it was to become a preacher.

My grandfather was a believing man, more so perhaps on Sunday than on other days. On weekdays he was quite earthy, which strangely seemed not to be a contradiction in him. I can still conjure vivid images of him wearing his dark wool suit and his black Stetson hat, leaving the farmstead with his buggy and team of sorrel ponies to go to church in the town. When he died and his earthly treasure was divided among us, the black Stetson passed on to me. It was my sole material inheritance from him. How it came to me, I don't know. It could have been that of my brothers and me, mine was the only head literally large enough to accommodate it. It is also possible that none of them wanted it. That I don't remember.

I like to believe the black hat was, in a way, the passing of his mantra on to me. He, too, had spent hours in the fields tilling and thinking. He would say, "I have been thinking and have come to believe." And I have come to think that it is OK for thinking people to believe. Unfortunately, my experience has been that university professors are expected to avoid the impression of intellectual inadequacy that is thought to attend interest in matters of belief.

While no thoughtful person would seriously contend that society doesn't derive some benefit from professors' answers to new questions, I am inclined to wonder if their efforts to answer ancient questions have long passed the point of diminishing returns. I am impressed with the scientific enlightenment about how the material world works, but I am disappointed in the current confusion of intellectual schemes in that other intellectual arena, which proposes to explore the meaning of human existence.

Who's to be blamed for this state of affairs? Could be the preachers, but the majority of citizens pay little attention to them. Perhaps it is the politicians' fault, but it is difficult to ascertain what, if anything, they do. Besides, society doesn't trust them − it only elects them. We professors must be at fault. After all, are not professors the experts about almost everything?

And do we not live in a society that turns to its experts for direction? Everything, it seems, except in matters of belief.

I can't believe God in His wisdom commissioned professors to make the rules governing what is believable. Sometimes I wonder if there are any rules. If there are, I have trouble with the presumption that it is the prerogative of professors to fashion them. Many professors leave the impression that is exactly what they are doing – despite dodging matters of belief.

There is no end to the writing predicated on the premise that we humans do, indeed, have capacity to understand the intangibles of the human soul. I submit it may be acceptable to believe that, but I am becoming increasingly fearful (when we eventually do understand) it won't be at all what we expect or want it to be. It may require us to believe some things we can't know. And the present state of intellectual affairs is that we already know more than we understand.

A persistent preoccupation with the nature of life and death pervades the history of human thought – that is, the ancient questions about why we are here and where we are going when we leave. Our age is no different, except that our technological ability to manipulate the processes of life and the event of death may cause us to think we have better answers to questions about life and death. Judging from the persistence of the questions, it would seem the answers are still elusive.

The very idea of new answers implies that present answers don't satisfy. Perhaps having no new answers more precisely describes my dilemma and my expectation that there should be some. Is it possible that the nature of being (or for that matter the nature of not being) is beyond knowing? That thought can be at once both comforting and frightening. Frightening in that we may be destined to existence in a state of uncertainty about why we exist. Comforting in the sense that answers don't change anything. We will continue to exist (for awhile at least) regardless of why we think we do.

I didn't become a preacher. I wanted new answers to the old questions. I became a professor of biology with the expectation that some insight about mental mechanisms of belief might be helpful. The realization that my professorial specialty hasn't given me new answers ought to be reason enough to stop writing. But I have observed that not having answers (especially to these questions) has never deterred professors from writing. I am still curious about why we insist on new answers to questions that may have none.

It seems that since we humans first became conscious of existence we have been reluctant to abandon the idea that it must mean something. *Why am I here?* is a persistent question that most humans don't have to be prompted to ask. In fact, the survival of religions seems to be sustained by the anticipation that humans, sooner or later, will ask that question. Persons raised on religious instruction, as I was, are quite likely provided with answers before it occurs to them to ask the question.

To be curious is intrinsically characteristic of all complex animals. It is what they are curious about that distinguishes them. While it is in the essence of humanness to ask questions, it is our insistence upon asking this one question that interests me. I am just as curious at the moment about why we keep asking this question as I am about any particular answer to it. That all our interrogation of the world suggests it is devoid of meaning doesn't seem to diminish our need to ask the question. It simply persists.

Does our being have to have meaning in some grander scheme? I believe it is OK to believe that it does. So did my grandfather.

Idea Merchants

Every ideology has its following of devotees - no matter whether the philosophy is as far ranging as evolution or as limited as that of the flat-earth society. Great political, religious, and philosophical *isms* have claimed the minds, even the lives of multitudes throughout history. Since the invention of alphabets and writing, scholars have aligned with the pros or cons of these ideological scenarios. The majority of civilization's accumulated mass of words has been devoted to recording, refining, and defending these inventions of the mind — or contrarily critiquing or discrediting opposing beliefs. The magnitude of this colossal collection of words is difficult to comprehend. Tending civilization's repository of intellectual artifacts has perennially consumed the time and energy of scholars and professors.

Contemporary culture with its crowds of ideologues is no different. Few societies (other than modern, first-world, developed countries) have the discretionary resources to support an enormous army of idea warriors managing ideological minutiae — most of which is trivial and does little to lessen the burdens of needy people. With the exception of writing fiction, defense of ideological territory is what most scholarly activity is about. (Actually the latter activity frequently resorts to its own kind of fiction.) The number of words expended in some of these major battles is astonishing.

The maintenance of this GCIP — gross cultural intellectual product — of course, is sustained by the trafficking in this commerce of ideas by scholars and professors often, unfortunately, under the guise of education. It's the stuff of which professors' jobs and reputations are made and is what the business of the academy is all about. This is the economy in which I invested my professional life. I learned, as professors must, to rummage about in this wealth of words seeking inspiration and enlightenment, to stay conversant, and to steer my students around the endless profusion of inconsequential trivia. The latter is not as easy as it may seem.

An interesting spin-off of this commerce of ideas is the clever marketing of one's intellectual obsession. It is not uncommon for a constituency of citizens (scholars and students included) to become so addicted to an idea that they are simply unable or unwilling to abandon it. Withdrawal threatens their entire worldview. Catering to these passionate allegiances becomes a lucrative means to exploit not only an idea but also an intellectually vulnerable constituency — a patronage often indifferent to or unaware of competing scenarios.

Lucky is the professor who discovers an audience in the reading public already so deeply devoted to an ideology that they have no inclination to consider alternatives. That allegiance can be exploited more often by discrediting opposing views — accurately or honestly, it doesn't matter — or by dismissing folks who hold contrary or alternative positions rather than by presenting convincing arguments for reasonable alternatives. A market can easily be created for books which tell readers why they should not think in the context of another philosophy, thereby relieving them of any need to seriously re-examine their fidelity to their own comfortable ideological convictions. Unfortunately, it is easier to reinforce an unexamined position than it is to convince someone of the merit of alternatives. (I suppose that is the perennial challenge of both formal education and the edification of the general public.)

I would like to be convinced that most Idea Merchants are motivated by concern for the intellectual, spiritual, and psychological welfare of their readers and not the commercial exploitation of intellectually vulnerable citizens. But I am still struggling to know if my sadness about this blatant exploitation of innocent readers is due to righteous indignation on their behalf, or that I wasn't smart enough to discover and market my own best-selling notions about why the dogma of contemporary biology is not good for the soul.

Divine Diversion

About the time I had mastered the practice and protocols of the professoriate, I received an ironic and unexpected invitation from a small rural congregation of cattle ranchers and wheat growers to become their pastor. Inasmuch as I had been a guest of the congregation on several occasions, I was already acquainted with these folks. They were my kind of people in whose presence I could revisit my early fantasies about farming, which I had abandoned at the age of twenty-seven to go to college – ironically to become a preacher.

The request was not without credibility. My first several college semesters were dedicated to becoming a preacher where I had learned some things about religious paradigms and that perspective on truth. But I abandoned that study disquieted about the dissonance between knowing and believing. Professors need to know. Preachers need to believe. I wanted to know.

Nevertheless, the invitation was seductive. The experience would put me in touch with folks who had realized my boyhood aspirations. Yet, I was a card-carrying, reductionist biology professor, the species about whom many churchgoers are most suspicious. I was comfortable spending my days learning about and marveling at the awesome cellular and molecular intricacies of living matter. But now — wary of God's sense of humor and amused at the thought that I might be anybody's spiritual leader — I was challenged to turn my attention to the mysterious intangibles of living souls.

Moreover, I was untrained in the art of preaching, unskilled at comforting the ill and saddened, unaccustomed to cautioning the wayward, or affirming the kind deeds and good will of parishioners. It seemed presumptuous of me to acquire these skills at their expense, so I declined the call with the provision that I would fill the role until they could find a person truly prepared for the task.

Seven years later the congregation had long abandoned their search. I had become their preacher. I submit that over time I learned how to preach (not the same as professing), to visit the ill, eulogize the departed, comfort the saddened, marry the young, caution the wayward, and affirm the kind deeds and good will of the faithful. None of which are assignments on the job description of a molecular biology professor. And all the while I continued during the week to present arguments to my students for the expediency of a worldview predicated on the dogma of contemporary biology.

While I never allowed myself to wonder aloud to my parishioners whether I had served them well, I was quick to acknowledge what they did for me. Their embrace, encouragement, hospitality, affirmation, and gracious goodwill enriched my professional and personal well being beyond all expectation. Seldom did they seem impressed or intimidated by my professorial credentials. Not only did they faithfully listen to my sermons, they invited me to help (or to believe I was helping) with their ranching activities. I operated their field machinery, worked the round up and other cattle chores, assisted with building projects, fought wildfires, and mended fences – the latter two pastoral activities in both meanings of the word.

All of this at the expense, my professional colleagues would say, of my reputation in the society of professional biologists. Summers and weekends, they warned me, were for immersing oneself in the minutiae and extending the margins of one's ideological niche.

Learning to function in an ideological posture quite different from that which all my training and degrees imposed upon me – while perhaps not professionally expedient – was delightfully liberating. No longer could I promote my chosen discipline as the only perspective on how to best understand existence with the same arrogance with which I had become comfortable.

A serious sojourn in the terrain of someone else's set of ideas will probably do much to subdue the subjectivity with which we experts are prone to defend the ideological high ground of our favored fields. I believe that academe would be well served by humanity professors spending a few summers in the labs of their colleagues in science.

At most educational institutions the preferred sabbatical activity is research. One wonders why professors – who already know more than they understand – continue to insist that merit accrues only to those who choose to submerge themselves further in the trivia of their ideological turfdom. Unfortunately, the incentive structure of the academic workplace precludes advancement in the absence of research. Beyond affording me a different ideological context in which to ponder my importance in the great scheme of things, this diversion delivered me from the delusion that being full of one's subject, i.e., full professor, is better than reserving head space for another perspective.

Naïvely, I suppose, but seldom did I worry about my professional reputation as I traveled by the wheat fields and ranch land on my way to proclaim biblical truths at the little church. I did, however, wonder if my long-ago-sainted, farmer grandfather was watching. He never called me *The Preacher*.

Molecular Me

Being a professor can isolate one from the real world. Not only do professors live in the world of ideas, they become passionate in their allegiance to them. Consequently, many become intellectually isolated from the realm of real things. Fortunately, as a professor of biology I was able to retain some contact with the real world. The domain of biology is (or was at one time) the world of real living things. However, the acclaimed professors of biology — the ones who get paid the most — have managed to reduce the phenomenon of life to an endless series of abstractions about molecules. That's the stuff of which Nobel Prizes are made.

I'm troubled by the number of biologists who have lost contact with the world of living things, like frogs and bugs and trees and humans. I grew up with horses, cows, pigs, turkeys, chickens, ducks and geese. Our farm had them all. We raised corn, wheat, oats, rye, and vegetables. In college the persistence of my boyhood fascination with these crops and critters caused me to gravitate away from the study of ideas and center my attention on living things.

That was long before DNA became the central theme of biology. I still wonder whether DNA is an abstraction or a thing. Perhaps it is both. As the science of biology and my participation in it evolved, I became intrigued with the notion that the secrets of life lay entangled in the busyness of molecules. So I moved into the arena of molecular biology, although reluctantly, fearful of losing sight of real organisms – the context in which the molecules are found doing their thing. But I became comfortable with molecular models of nerve cell activity or schemes about how gene information is translated into exquisite three-dimensional structures.

While I continue to be intrigued by the incomprehensible complexities of cells and intricate molecular mechanisms, I struggle not to lose sight of organisms – the *context* where, in reality, all creatures live. But that reality retreats in the face of the accumulating minutiae about molecules at work. I begin to wonder which is the mirage, my molecules or me. I cannot be content with the thought that I am no more than Nature's way of perpetuating a peculiar set of molecules. I prefer to think of the whole of me as the purpose of my molecular parts rather than the whole of me as a means to an end for my molecules.

Over time the poorly charted connection between the isolated activities of molecules and the symphonic totality of life became the focus of my intellectual curiosity about the nature of humanness. Ironically, that very curiosity occurs only in combinations of specific molecules exquisitely arranged in elaborate organismal complexes – like professors and students. There is no mystery apart from the molecules, but the mystery is not *in* the molecules. It is the whole, not the parts, that asks the questions. That is significant!

What does it mean to be human in the dogma of molecular biology? Molecular biology *per se* knows little about and seems impotent to address what matters most to me as I experience life - the confluence of bitter & sweet, pain & pleasure, joy & grief, harmony & dissonance and the perception of beauty, evil, freedom, justice, morality, immortality, sacrifice, and tragedy.

These experiences do not transpire apart from the molecular and cellular goings-on in organisms, yet they all evaporate in the face of reductionist methodology, which fails to find them in the isolated parts. Paradoxically, this very useful methodology obscures as much as it enlightens. It is what gets left out or is unaccounted for that causes this professor's disenchantment. We know so much more than we understand.

No informed person will deny that molecular biology has produced enormously useful insights about the phenomenon of life. Indeed, exploring the enchantments of molecular biology was demanding, exhilarating, and an intellectually rewarding exercise. I had hoped the journey would eventually bring me to a clearer understanding of life and especially of its manifestation in the totality of human experience – which was why I went to college in the first place. Now I am not so sure. I am nagged by a growing suspicion that molecular biology moves us in the wrong direction. I am going back to the farm and think about it.

Probabilities

Well into the eighth decade of life I am now persuaded that much of life just happens. Statisticians assign probability values (a model academic exercise) to single events assumed to be random. They, then, by compounding probabilities, will predict the chances that anyone chosen at random will succumb to cancer, die in an airliner crash, succeed in college, live to the age of seventy-five, or become a professor. Following this reasoning and compounding the probabilities of steps in the process, e.g. bachelor, masters and doctoral degrees, brings one to the conclusion that professors are statistically quite improbable. Yet they happen.

How it happens is more readily understood than why it happens. The path to professordom, although not officially proscribed, is quite standard. Generally one obtains a sequence of academic degrees culminating with a doctorate. Although a Ph.D. is a prerequisite for many university faculty positions and for upper academic ranks, it is nowhere written that having obtained a Ph.D. degree obligates one to become a professor. On the other hand, the majority of persons having earned an academic doctoral degree are professors. One wonders which is cause and which is effect. It has been written (somewhere in this volume) that after the degree there's not much else to do. Have you noticed how frequently having been written makes something true?

I asked my most favorite philosopher, a loveable but eccentric guy, if he was a professor because he held a Ph.D. or did he have the degree because he was a professor. "Does an apple tree grow apples because it's an apple tree or is it an apple tree because it grows apples?" he asked, restating the question in typical philosopher fashion. Then he said, "Probably they just happen." Whether he meant apples or professors, it was a strange answer since philosophy claims to have the corner on certainty, i.e. a probability of 1.00. That both apples and professors are random events subject to statistical analysis was a new idea for me.

So I began to wonder what series of random circumstances might factor in one's decision to become a professor. And how does one arrive at the probability for each factor contributing to the outcome? Suppose someone was told he or she would look good in a mortarboard hat. How does one assign a probability to that? Whatever that probability is, how it influences one's ambition to become a professor should be reduced by the probability that mortarboard hats enhance the aesthetic countenance of very few professors.

Yet judging from the animation displayed by professors wearing mortarboard hats, one becomes suspicious that most are not dissuaded by that low probability. The rather small number of opportunities a professor has to legitimately display his or her academic accouterments should argue against those occasions being a significant factor leading one into the profession.

The observation that most professors seldom decline invitations to parade their heady credentials tends to argue otherwise. There must be a researcher somewhere studying the distinction between professors wearing hats and hats wearing professors. By the way, I still have my academic headdress which I wear ceremoniously on occasion – but with a newfound modesty engendered by the realization that it doesn't say as much as I once thought.

A circumstance that has been said to steer persons toward the profession (the probability of which I don't know) is that they were unpopular in high school which drove them to take refuge in books. It doesn't inevitably follow that every friendless kid who is attracted to books will become a professor. Yet when unpopular kids come to college already having discovered the excitement of books, they will probably retreat deeper into the refuge of ideas and may already be on the path to professordom. I can't remember any of my professor colleagues ever bragging about having been chosen *most popular* by their high school classmates.

I went through high school quite unnoticed. Not so in college. Ten years older than my first year contemporaries with noticeably graying hair, I was an improbable presence in Sociology 101 - Intro to College Life. I moved freely among the students who were never quite certain whether I was one of them or one of the professors. It was quite freeing and (except for attending classes) I functioned quietly on the edges of collegiate excitement. That's where

I discovered the library. It is easy to hide in the library, but one does not have to be friendless to take refuge in books. A sincere love of books is not restricted to introverts.

My attraction to books had little to do with my becoming a professor. I was mature enough when I matriculated to suspect that the essence of education was more than learning how to do something, i.e. learning how to teach, or to practice law or medicine, much less how to be a professor. My fascination for words, ideas, and books grew out of the discovery that intellectual quest was more exciting in itself than as a means to become a professor. I recall a doctoral student friend of mine yearning for the time "when this degree thing is over so that I can get on with my education," he said.

The probability of an 18 year-old (self-esteem not withstanding) starting college intent on becoming a professor is quite low. During four decades of meeting students seeking advice about career choices, not once did I hear one state a desire to become a professor. The absence of pre-professor curricula suggests that becoming a professor is rarely premeditated and is, therefore, a random event.

Professors are no less diverse than any other group engaged in a single vocation. Oh, yes, they all like to talk, think they can write, enjoy books, prefer to sit, like to be seen and wear goofy hats to enhance visibility. In the population at large each of those predilections — except the hats — is quite common. It's the combination of them all under one hat that's improbable. But it's what makes a professor. By the way, I think I look pretty good in my gold-tasseled mortarboard hat.

The Right Not to Write

Sooner or later (usually sooner) we professors encounter persons who automatically assume we will have written something. Professors are clearly expected to write, but the expectations about that anticipated writing are quite nebulous. Writing motivated by the expectation of others will likely not be good writing, nor should the writer expect those who expected it to read it. I once wrote a short essay on request, which subsequently appeared in a local publication. I really didn't expect anyone to read it, but I didn't anticipate being hurt to discover that no one did.

Unfortunately, the writing of professors may not be precipitated by professors having all that much to say. What beginner in the business has not succumbed to the notion that professors instinctively know how to write – only to demonstrate, by doing so, that it is not necessarily true? There's a blurb in Proverbs that paraphrases something like this: *"It is much better not to write and cause folks to wonder if you can, than to write and remove all doubt."*

Unhappily, status in the profession precludes doing otherwise. Recognition or status is difficult to achieve apart from of the rules of the game. Still one wonders why more don't choose to perish. That would do more for the intellectual landscape than to publish solely to avoid perishing. Fortunately for the survivors, much of their stuff is not widely read. Yet it is amazing how writing, which receives no acclaim and perhaps deserves none, continues to accumulate.

The ability to write does not, by itself, establish that one should. The presumption that professors know how to write is often shrouded by the more persistent notion that to be a good professor one must write. One wonders why, if professors are so smart, the notion that writing *per se* merits recognition has not met with more resistance. Ought not some recognition be given to those who realize that they have nothing to say and refrain from doing so? Ironically, in keeping with the rules of the game, one would probably be expected to justify in writing one's decision not to write.

Having nothing to say seems to characterize about as many professors who write as it does professors who don't. My grandfather would say, "Quiet people aren't the only one's who don't say much." Surely you have noticed how frequently having nothing to say fails to deter writers. Actually the number of words employed by those who have nothing to say (to say what it is they have nothing to say something about) is amazing. And some do it so well that one suspects they do it intentionally.

A common professorial practice is to write about the writing of others. It's called research. To write with authority about the writing of others one has to read a lot, preferably the writing about which one intends to write. It takes considerable skill to write about what someone has written without betraying the fact that one didn't read it. I am not yet that clever, so I think I will write about not writing.

Obviously one cannot write about what someone has not written. One can, however, write about someone not having written anything. Frequently this is done in defense of not writing.

There is much to be said for not writing. Not writing (like not speaking) keeps others guessing. But once have written something, one is bared to challenge, to criticism, and possibly to embarrassment. On the other hand, not writing entails no such danger yet is not totally without challenge. Without their writing to critique, non-writers are open to assault from another direction. In academic circles non-writers are gently chided about not writing. And who among those of us who don't write is not irked by the innuendo that not having written something is evidence that we can't.

There is a subtle seduction which I have avoided until now. It is tempting to assume that encouragement to write means someone believes you have something worth saying. It has been said that there are two kinds of writers: those who write and those who know enough not to. In fact, it was I who said it once when I was asked why I hadn't written any books.

Now it seems to me that there may actually be four categories of folks when it comes to writing. There are: (1) those who should write and do, (2) those who should not write but do, (3) those who should write but don't, and (4) those who should not write and don't. My having done this piece now places me in either the first or second of those groups.

One could make this a typical academic exercise and write at length about those four categories. For example, one might wonder why there are (among those who do write) so many that should not. Furthermore, one might want to know whether those who really shouldn't write (and don't) don't write because they know that they shouldn't. If true, that seems to me to be commendable.

However, for me to write any more about writing (or not writing) might be more than many of you care to read. If it seems that I write irreverently, you are right. It is because through the years I have read a lot that I wouldn't have needed to. Paradoxically, much of it was so well written I was enticed to read it all, only to discover it didn't have that much to say. Those of you who have read this piece to the end will have been there too.

Student Teachers

Sooner or later, professors, like all professionals, must reckon with retirement and life after college — life with no classes, no tests, no grades, no deans, no faculty meetings, and no students. For me all of that except the *no students* part has been delightful. After decades of preparing for classes, creating and grading tests, agonizing over final grades, the challenge of avoiding faculty meetings, and scrambling for promotion — I yearn for none of that. But I do become quite pensive when I contend with the absence of students to instruct me about being young and hopeful. Now there are no more new students — only the memories of former students who gave me reason to be glad about having been a professor for the past forty years.

Retirement meant moving out of my campus office. I was quite surprised to discover how little of what I had accumulated was worth saving. I saved my file of memos from the many deans in whose training I had a part, my collection of biophilosophy books, as well as the notes, letters, and especially the memories of students. I am convinced that after forty years of college life on the campus, in the classroom, in the lab, and in the office what will endure will be memories of my students who taught me well, which now in retrospect appears to have been all of them.

My very first professorial appointment came about suddenly and unexpectedly. At that moment all of my previous academic endeavors had been preparation for an assignment with a foreign missions agency. Unwilling to accept the agency's censorship of my correspondence with their constituency, I was dismissed and free to find other ways to exploit my recently acquired credentials. The public schools were an option, but they were in session and their faculty rosters fixed. While wondering what to do next, I received a phone call from a person I didn't know at a California university about which I knew little more than the prowess of its basketball team.

Could I come and teach biology at his university, the man asked. There was urgency in his voice as he continued, "Classes begin next week." Five days later I stood before my very first class of college student scholars who sat with pens and pencils poised ready to record the punditry of this rookie professor.

This first semester I was assigned four classes, three of which were laboratory courses, whose enrollments included a half dozen of the brightest, intimidating undergraduates of all my teaching experience. Fortunately, they were also some of the most sensitive and helpful students I have known. It was a challenging, serendipitous, but brutal introduction to the professoriate. My most recent previous teaching experience had been a one-year stand in junior high school.

One of my professors had made it safe to say he didn't know by quickly adding, ". . . and I don't think anyone else does either." These students wouldn't let me leave it there. They allowed me to say I didn't know but wouldn't permit me to be comfortable not knowing. I learned from them to know when they knew I didn't know.

When some of his students rained on his parade of facts an impatient colleague grumbled, "Teaching would be delightful work if it weren't for the students." Students do indeed get in the way of some professors. Not all professors catch on that professing to students is not about the professor nor his or her profusion of facts. Students have the same access to information as their professors. The alert students (which are eventually at one time or another all of them) are curious about the professors' interpretation of their accretion of facts. Education is not about what the professor knows, it is about students wanting to know *why* what the professor knows is worth knowing.

Of course, not every student will buy into a prof's particular paradigmatic twist on the data. "What's the story here?" my better students would ask, or "Why is your story better than any other?" One of my students wrote, *"This class is a waist of time and your ideas are a bunch of carp!"* Not the most sophisticated expression of discontent, but I was alerted to his having heard my facts and his displeasure with what I was making them say. My task was not to correct his spelling. (That's why we have English professors.) Mine was to engage him in conversation about his disquiet and ascertain what story he thought lay embedded in the data.

Too often professors spend their time and that of their students giving them answers to questions that have not yet occurred to them. The questions for which the prof is providing answers are quite likely not the most pressing concerns for students facing an unknown future where the prof's answers may seem irrelevant.

Getting students to ask their questions is the perennial challenge of classroom teaching. I can't recall the number of class sessions I began with the question, "How may I help you today?" only to be met with studied silence. But eventually a student uncomfortable with the quiet would ask a question and the class was off to an effective session. Indeed, the transition from the prof's questions to those of liberated students is the start of effective teaching. In retrospect, I believe the silent moments while I waited for the students to sign on were the most profitable investment of my time and theirs.

It was a long time ago, but I can remember being told in grade school to quit interrupting with questions and listen. (Maybe that's why my grandfather called me *The Perfesser*.) It didn't occur to my teacher that my curiosity had been aroused and she failed to exploit that. Alert students' questions, not about *what* I said but *why* I said what I said, were invaluable. My students taught me to know the difference. Students deserve to know the significance of the flow of facts being disgorged. That's more important than staying on schedule with the syllabus. I could produce an impressive syllabus but usually abandoned it when it became apparent that the agenda was getting in the way. Dispensing data is the function of books. And getting to the end of the book is not what matters. One should not wonder why students so frequently resort to regurgitation during examination. There ought to be some reason for students and professors being in the classroom at the same time. What matters is whether any intellectual intercourse has occurred.

Few students sleep through the end of a class session. In fact, it is then when many of them are most alert. Too often it is the professor who is the last to recognize that the point of diminishing results had long passed. One of the reasons for my limited success as a preacher was that I learned early to stop talking before the congregation stopped listening. That skill was exceedingly useful in the lecture hall. Only the students were much less subtle than the parishioners in the liveliness with which they indicated it was all over. Generally students manifest considerable tolerance for redundancy, but that tolerance wanes quickly as they begin to notice when the lecturer has missed all the best opportunities to stop. It was not always the clock that indicated the session was over. The clicking sound of thirty ring-binder notebooks snapping shut is a signal difficult to ignore.

I am not as impressed with the ancient Greeks as are my philosopher friends. But I do recall hearing about one for whom an ideal educational scenario was two people on a log with nothing between them to preclude contact between their minds. I like that. My most memorable and productive pedagogical sessions occurred in my office when curious students stopped by to chat. Plagued by a pernicious tendency to procrastinate all my professional life, I intentionally solicited distraction by leaving my office door open that perchance a student might walk in and offer some respite from the tedium of grading papers or committee reports. Conversations with inquisitive students on the other end of my pedalogue often revealed what, if any, intellectual independence my classroom style was generating. That is what education is all about.

One of my wisest education professors when giving advice about teaching said, "Be on the alert for students who are smarter than you are; learn how to recognize them and then don't try to help them– just stay out of their way." Perhaps I should have done that. But I decided that when I encountered bright students I would stand close by and let their brilliance reflect on me, thereby leaving the impression that I was contributing to it. I hope it worked. I still indulge in the fantasy that I had something to do with the success of my students.

I do sometimes wonder whether the intellectual maturation of my students might have been better served by my writing books. The incentive structure of the academy favors those who write books. But it doesn't seem to consider the intellectual well being of those for whom it was intended to serve. This book is for them.

Acknowledgements

At the risk of shifting the blame for this book, I wish to acknowledge the contribution of all who traveled with me during my four-decade sojourn in the land of letters – classmates, students, professors, colleagues, and yes, deans. Without their wise council, kind affirmation, gentle encouragement, intellectual inspiration and overall goodwill, I probably would have retreated to the farm.

I am especially indebted to my students whose wisdom, insights, questions, energy, hope, and youthful enthusiasm sustained and gave direction and meaning to my professorial adventure.

A special thanks to Pauline for the picture – worth more than a thousand words.

I am exceptionally fortunate and immensely grateful for my family without whose love, grace and patience this book would still be reverie. Pat's tenacious professional editing smoothed out the writing and exposed the meaning of the words. Suzanne's candid critique, creative design, and imaginative format enhance the reading. Her sincere enthusiasm and encouragement stilled my epidsodes of doubt. Beth's affectionate affirmation, keen sense of subtlety, and ready response to the humor made it all fun.

I am sincerely grateful.